RELIGIOUS CONVERSION AND PERSONAL IDENTITY

RELIGIOUS CONVERSION AND PERSONAL IDENTITY:

How and Why People Change

V. BAILEY GILLESPIE

Religious Education Press
Birmingham   Alabama

Library of Congress Cataloging in Publication Data

Gillespie, Virgil Bailey.
  Religious conversion and personal identity.

  Includes bibliographical references and index.
  1. Conversion—Psychology. 2. Identification
(Religion) I. Title.
BR110.G53   248'.24   79-15605
ISBN 0-89135-018-7

Religious Education Press, Inc.
1531 Wellington Road
Birmingham, Alabama 35209
10 9 8 7 6 5 4 3 2

*Religious Education Press publishes books and educational materials exclusively
in religious education and in areas closely related to religious education. It is
committed to enhancing and professionalizing religious education through the
publication of significant scholarly and popular works.*

PUBLISHER TO THE PROFESSION

DEDICATION

TO MOMENTS OF QUIET REFLECTION,
AND EAR LOBES, WITHOUT WHICH
THERE WOULD BE NO CHURCH.

I Corinthians 11–13

CONTENTS

PREFACE

I have always been fascinated by the experience called "conversion." From the first time I heard a preacher intoning his "call" for all to come to the Lord until today, when I have students relating their "conversion" experiences, I have found the process of religious change most interesting. In my life a reorientation of life goals and a commitment developed through theological reflection has occurred which some would call religious conversion. That commitment has, through later reinterpretation and clarification, become a deep concern for the Christian purpose in the world. Therefore, I have a degree of personal interest in this topic.

Further whetting my interest in this type of relational study has been my observation of many within whom has occurred this quest for identity and uniqueness and sense of completeness with the same orientation in fact and the same dynamics in operation as in conversion. Earlier work on glossolalia and religious experience contributed to this focus of attention.

People experience many types of changes during a lifetime, but most compelling to study are those deep alterations which form the fabric of life out of which action comes and personality is framed. Both the experiences of religious conversion and personal identity formation have profound effects on the style of life and the actual perception of the importance of life. Before anyone can make a success of living and working—creating, selling, teaching, ministering—basic questions concerning the existence of life, the value of life and all involved in life, the direction and motivation of life need resolution.

The motivations for change are myriad: social, familial, theological, philosophical, pathological, emotional. Even a religious conversion type of change can have origins other than spiritual.

Implications for religious educators and counselors become obvious when we probe the unique experiences of religious conversion and personal identity to see their actual changing power, to see their close resemblance in style and feeling tone, and to probe their similarities and effects on the life. People who change, be it dramatically or ever so gradually, people who find themselves and identify with God, begin to be creative and fulfilled. They find a kind of internal calm amid the perplexities of a troublesome time and world. The options to change and respond are the qualities of personal religion, while the temptations to stabilize and solidify are the limitations of institutionalized religion. The dynamics of religion are the foci of change.

The substance of this book was developed in interchanges with Allen J. Moore, Paul Irwin, and Donald McNassor in discussions about the experiences of conversion and identity. An examination of the material extant concerning these two experiences revealed that most work in this area centered around the famous studies of James, Starbuck, and Leuba, completed early in the century. To all these men I owe a personal debt for initial stimulation.

Family structures come under stress during times of concentrated endeavor and personal reflection, and kudos must go to Judith, my wife, an already busy court reporter, who added this manuscript to her proofing and editing tasks.

It is impossible to begin a work like this without some presuppositions. I assume the activity of God in the lives of men and in their world. God is active, he is revealing Himself, he is acting in history and in the lives of man. Christians have confused God's actions with man's response, however. Perhaps God is a greater respector of persons than we had imagined, and man is allowed to respond in kind to the factors which nudge change. This book examines this relationship and explores these two concepts lived out in experience—religious conversion and personal identity.

V. BAILEY GILLESPIE, Ph.D.
Riverside, California

CHAPTER I

CONVERSION: A Way to Change

"... To have a conversion experience is nothing much. The real thing is to be able to keep on taking it seriously; to retain a sense of its plausibility ..." Peter L. Berger.

The concern of this book is religious conversion, that form of religious expression so much studied by psychologists of religion, preachers of righteousness, evangelists, and experienced by way-out Jesus Freaks, apostles, prophets, presidential candidates, and men of God. This experience is claimed to be central to the religious change of an individual. Religious conversion is that siritual encounter equated with the experience alluded to by Jesus of Nazareth in his evening answer to Nicodemus regarding his authority. "Verily, verily, I say unto thee, except a man be born again, he cannot see the kingdom of God."[1] The focus of this book then is how individuals change in that area of their inmost lives that touch the holy.

Conversion is most commonly understood to be a dramatic religious experience. Perhaps the violence and emotionalism usually attributed to this event has caused it to be so central in most studies of religious experience. The topic is not usually analyzed in its social setting. Because of its subjective nature it has had little respect from those individuals who are interested in religious phenomena, since it is assumed to be supernatural by most religious

1

groups. It therefore lies outside the realm of their investigation. The secular experience, on the other hand, such as identity, has been given considerable discussion of a more psychological nature. Since this kind of human change can be readily attributed to many sources, it has been discussed much more analytically. Yet religious conversion experience has had its problems being considered an acceptable topic for any study at all.

Walter Houston Clark comments that conversion is "a sort of psychological slum, to be avoided by any really respected scholar,"[2] while George Jackson suggests that the subject belongs in that realm in which our minds do not easily move, an area in which we find ourselves a kind of alien. "When we hear of conversions we think immediately of revivals and the clatter of machinery which always jars upon our nerves: to us revivalism is another name for hysteria and unwholesome excitement."[3] It is also true that most of the literature about conversion, religious experience, and psychology of religion is uncritical and riddled with personal opinion. This makes an understanding of this experience even more difficult. And since many bizarre and unorthodox forms of religious expression are extant today and are in many ways on the increase, this too adds to the problem of understanding conversion's nature. There seems, as well, to be something embarrassing about discussing religious experience at all.

Nevertheless, this topic deserves probing and understanding, and some relationships shown with its secular counterpart—identity. It is not the purpose of this book to debate whether or not conversions take place, for the experience is well documented in history. Too many cases have been cited, such as the apostle Paul on the road to Damascus, to have to debate whether or not such occurrences actually take place. William James, after courting some forceful, sudden conversion stories, says,

> I might multiply cases almost indefinitely, but these will suffice to show you how real, definite, and memorable an event a sudden conversion may be to him who has the experience. Throughout the height of it he undoubtedly seems to himself a passive spectator, or undergoer of an astounding process performed upon him from above. There is too much evidence of this for any doubt of it to be possible.[4]

John Wesley gives many examples of converts healed in soul and body in a moment.[5] St. Augustine's appraisal illustrates the definiteness of this experience where he says, "For immediately I had reached the end of this sentence it was as though my heart was filled with a light of confidence and all the shadows of my doubt were swept away."[6] Much more is known and documented regarding the mystical conversion of Pascal. He was typical in that he was a very devout type before his conversion experience. Before he was twenty-four years old, he is reported to have been enlightened by God through the reading of books of piety so that he understood perfectly what the Christian was supposed to do, yet he experienced another religious conversion at thirty years of age. He describes the experience on a piece of paper found over his heart at his death.

> The year of grace 1954. Monday November the 23rd. . . . From about half past ten in the evening to about half past midnight, Fire.
>
> God of Abraham, God of Isaac, God of Jacob. Not of the philosophers and of the learned. Certainty. Certainty. Feeling. Joy. Peace. God of Jesus Christ. *Deum meum et Deum vestrum.* Thy God shall be my God—Forgetful of the world and of all

except God. One finds him only by the ways taught in the Gospel. Greatness of the human soul. Righteous Father, the world has not known thee, but I have known thee. Joy, joy, joy, tears of joy. . . . My God will you leave me? May I not be separated from thee eternally.

This is eternal life, knowing thee the only true God and the one sent by you J. C.—Jesus Christ. Jesus Christ. I have been separated from him: I have fled from him, renounced him, crucified him. May I never be separated from him.[7]

There is only fragmentary knowledge of what appears to have been a similar miraculous conversion experienced by St. Thomas Aquinas in 1273. He had led an actively religious life which culminated in his *Summa Theologica*. Then at age forty-eight he had an experience which inhibited further literary composition; he claimed: "I can write no more; for everything that I have written seems like straw, by comparison with the things I now see and which have been revealed to me."[8]

A more typical experience is that of Edward Hale's religious conversion, which was reported by Edwin Starbuck simply as growth.

. . . There had never been any dramatic, overwhelming religious crisis in his life. He had been brought up in a Christian home; since childhood he took it as a matter of course that he was to learn as much as he could about the world and was to do what he could to relieve the needs of others; all his life he had known and respected wise and intelligent men who were religious; and in spite of occasional doubts and questions, his own religious convictions had undergone a deepening and enriching through the years.[9]

The history of the world records great awakenings where conversional change took place. The great awakening in 1734–1750; Wesley's successes, 1740–1790; the reformations in Kentucky, 1796–1815; Nettelton's and Finney's revivals, 1828–1840; the revival of Millerism, 1840–1844; the American, Irish, and Welsh revivals in 1857–1959; and the revivals of Moody in the 1870–1880s—all exemplify the religious revivals of the era. Yet today, revival, with the accompanying phenomenon of conversion is still extant. The renewed interest by the Jesus Movements, Neo-Pentecostalism, Born-again Christians, and the charismatic renewal groups brings this issue again to the forefront in human experience.

And so, let us examine the religious experience, conversion.

RELIGIOUS EXPERIENCE

When one talks of conversion experience, one usually thinks of it as a religious experience. This necessitates an understanding of what is religious. Books have been written regarding just this, but to proceed without this concept understood would cause confusion at a later time. So, briefly, some comments to define "religious" are in order.

Definitions of religion and conversion are always in danger of being influenced by many of the same things—subjective standards or superficial manifestations. What some scholars label as content, others label form.[10] Others label "religious" such things as liturgy, belief, institutions, or even specific doctrines. What is here referred to as "religious" is that which, as Tillich asserts, is of ultimate concern.[11] It poses the aspect of a "unity of direction" that suggests man find in religious experience a unity of life and an answer to life's questions by a knowledge and understanding of God's ways. This God could be defined as Being, Other, or any of many terms used to describe the infinite. Yet conversion as a religious experience is an event that searches out those unifying qualities of existence which give meaning of ultimate value to one's life. In addition to this quality of "religious" is the sensing of divine presence as perceived by the experiencer.

The question "what is religious," is in itself the subject of thousands of pages. One cannot help but wonder if individual bias is what determines its definition. If one finds himself wondering about the feeling tones of knowing God, emphasis is on the personal piety and presence that transcends the mundane. For others, religion takes on a societal feel, with concerns about groups and how they learn, about responses, size, and growth in conformity with the known traditions of piety. Still another definition suggests the embodiment of the belief in the daily walks of the believers. This position regarding the lives of the faithful is so vague that "faith" loses content and response altogether. The general category of life as religion is perhaps too broad to examine.

John Westerhoff III suggests: "My understanding of *religion* refers to those concrete communal expressions of faith which are embodied in the life of a people—a community of faith. Religion is faith given shape, form, and content."[12]

This all-inclusive definition is comprehensive. Religion involves the belief, the feelings, the process of becoming, and the content of faith. This definition is tentative, yet useful for this book, for it gives a fuller understanding of the inclusiveness of life with God. It is not just the feelings when one encounters the divine, yet is it not that as well? Omitted, however, are the finer distinctions of the relationship of symbolism, superstition or hallucination, nor does this definition seek for the source of religious experience. Overlooked are the spokesmen who see religion as emphasizing the social aspects of life. Walter Clark's definition I find most useful in understanding religion when he says, "Religion can be most characteristically described as the inner experience of the individual when he senses a Beyond, especially as evidenced by the effects of this experience on his behavior when he actively attempts to harmonize his life with the Beyond."[13] This definition accurately portrays an important truth, as man in his inner experience tries to live his life in tune with the experience as he finds it. This does not rule out the definition that religion is defined as being those groups organized to accomplish the task of the mission of God as they perceive it. When religion is used to mean this fact, the context is explicit. The insight of Max Weber—that religion claims to offer an ultimate stand toward the world by virtue of a direct grasp of the world's meaning—is equally significant.[14]

"Experience" defined is simply, as Tillich referred to it, "the awareness of something that happens to somebody" or the "state of being grasped by the spiritual presence."[15] Some hold to the notion of a definite kind of experience which is itself religious, and make out of that experience something very unique, marked off from every other kind of experience. This confuses the issue. Rather, every experience, be it aesthetic, scientific, moral, or political, could have religious qualities. But "religious" as a quality of experience signifies something that may belong to all these experiences.[16] Therefore, all experiences are potentially religious and contain a possible religious dimension, since religion is a perspective on life and a quality given to the experience by one who experiences it.

The ancient Hebrew concept of man is helpful here. Ancient man was viewed as being close to God. He was incomplete as a person without this relationship of belonging to God. The stories of scripture suggest a wandering from God on the part of man. Even the first allusions in Genesis giving sin its rise in humanity through the separation of man from God illustrate this. The history of the Old Testament gives a picture of God and man attempting a reunion. Some unsuccessful attempts at finding God are thwarted by God himself because the source of reunion is from man himself rather than from God. The tower of Babel story is an excellent example of this kind of attempt.

Since ancient man viewed all things through this relational concept with God, no secular things existed. There was religious value in all of life itself. God was related in every way to life, and therefore to man himself. Faith was life. As man learned to love God he felt more a part of God. He began to feel a deeper sense of belonging, a deeper closeness developed, until Paul could illustrate his understanding of this concept by exclaiming, "For I am sure that neither death, nor life, nor angels, nor principalities, nor things present, nor things to come, nor powers, nor height, nor depth, nor anything else in all creation, will be able to separate us from the love of God in Christ Jesus our Lord."[17]

The popular picture of religious conversion experience, however, assumes that it is generally apart from more traditional religious forms, perhaps accompanied by various states of awareness and therefore dramatic and intense. If religious conversion is this, then it is no wonder that many do not try to define it or at least avoid it as some sort of pathology, as Leon Salzman does when he defines all religious conversion as a pathological condition described as "cosmic feelings, states of rapture, and mystical phenomena."[18]

Religious conversion, like any other human behavior, may be studied from all points of view—theological, philosophical, sociological, ethical, or psychological—and the definition of the subject in many ways reflects the purpose of the study and the orientation of the investigator. Such hampers the definition of conversion itself. The bewildering variety of definition of religious conversion reflects such relativities.

CONVERSION OR COLLAPSE

The word conversion has been variously defined. Its English root has many meanings which often depend upon the context in which the word is used. For example, it is usually referring to a "turning" or a "change from one state to another," such as the scientific conversion of water to ice. Those with a military bent find its usage describing a change of front exposed to attack, or the change of bore in firearms. In discussion, it is thought of as a change in viewpoint or belief from those previously held. In finance, it means a change of a security, currency, or coinage from one type to another. In legal circles, it is used in describing unlawful appropriation and use of another's belongings. In logic, it is the producing of a new proposition by transposing the subject and predicate of the original proposition. Those involved in mathematical science find in it a change in the form of a quantity or an expression without a change in the value.[19] The word is used to describe automobile tops and hide-a-beds, and in physics it is a process of converting raw material into energy. In these domains the term conversion has a more or less clearly-defined meaning. The basic connotation running throughout these technical usages is "change," "transformation," and "transposition."

Turning from the technical uses of the term, we find two other domains of help in understanding the English usage of the word. First, the word is used in a number of ordinary situations describing the action between people, beliefs and their attitudes; and secondly, in a religious sense, it is usually used in a religious way that is so vague it is barely definable. Those who believe that they are reflecting religious meanings when they use it are many, but because they have not defined the term, much confusion exists as to its precise meaning. For example, it is used as a noun: "Marge is a recent convert to this viewpoint." Here the noun usage means the person herself. There are no religious overtones at all. When used as a verb, however, as in "he spoke with such conviction and argued so energetically that I know he was trying to convert me," the meaning is to exert influence over someone and the change is something brought about by another. A third usage describes a more vague usage as it describes an experience. For example: "You do not need to labor this point, for you see, you are already speaking to the converted." Here a state of mind or experience is implied. It is not defined, and its vagueness is supposed to contain truth about experience. In the first two illustrations, the emphasis is on beliefs and viewpoints, but in the last, an experience is delineated.[20] The usage is clear, but the meaning is not. It is interesting to note that Argyle, in his work on religious conversion done in 1958, basing his study on McKeefery's review in 1949 of thirty-two studies of religious conversion experiences in the last half century, concluded that between ten and thirty percent of Americans experienced such crisis religious conversion and that the dominant age was about fifteen years. Yet in this study he failed to define the term conversion or to explain its relationship to change in adolescence.[21]

Thus, the English usage varies with context. It can be a change from Roman Catholicism to Buddhism, a shift in beliefs without a church, a lesser degree of change by situation, such as marriage or citizenship. Or it may mean the crisis in which a man comes to himself, as did the prodigal son when "for the first time (he) faces up to the realities of his moral and spiritual situation."[22] It may have the emotional connotations of the revival meeting where the preacher conjures up intense emotion or powers within the situation whereby one is "converted," or it may be simply the change that comes when one commits oneself to the best as he perceives it. It has theological overtones when it is a change of beliefs and implies an intellectual shift of viewpoint by thorough search, exploration, and insight, divine or human. It has emotional overtones when it comes through renewal in its deepest sense. The word has been used to describe change in affiliation of church membership as the word religion implies when referring to groups organized to work effectively; or it has a unique vagueness that comes from misuse and lack of clarity by meaning a religious experience one goes through. This lack of clarity is evidenced in the literature of conversion itself and becomes clearer as one studies this event in definitional usage. Yet when religious conversion is spoken of, usually one type crops into the imagination. The sudden form and the Pauline type have been taken as a standard by revivalists, and most people simply accept their dictum and visualize this form. Few have spoken out for other understandings of this word as strongly as George Cutten, when he said in 1908, "Not only is instantaneous conversion not the only true type of approaching God, but it is the extreme form of one type among several . . . it would be more true to say that no two persons ever come in the same way but each case is unique."[23] Clark suggests that for an English definition, conversion simply signifies a "turning about, a definite change of front, a passing from one state of being to an altogether different as a definite and specific act."[24] A study of the use of the word as used will aid in understanding the nature of this experience and in defining it.

BIBLICAL MODELS

The understanding of the word conversion centers around a few words in the Old and New Testaments. In Hebrew the word *shub* (שׁוּב) is used to express both the transitive and intransitive moods. The word means "to return" in a general sense and is found in the following passages: Psalm 51:13, "Sinners shall be converted unto thee"; Psalm 19:7, "The law of the Lord is perfect converting the soul";[25] Isaiah 1:27, "Zion shall be redeemed with judgments, and her converts with righteousness";[26] Isaiah 6:10, "Lest they see with their eyes and hear with their ears, and understand with their heart, and convert and be healed." The word is used in these passages in the active voice and in a neuter sense in all the above except Psalm 19:7, and might be as well rendered "return." It is frequently used with a second verb to give the sense of "again or back."[27] The Hebrew word *shub* occurs in the Old Testament some 1,146 times and means such things as (1) "to return," Genesis 18:33; (2) "to turn back," Judges 3:19; (3) "to return from a foreign land," Ruth 1:6; (4) "a turning around," I Kings 19:27; (5) "to turn in the course of action," II Kings 24:1; (6) "to turn from sin," I Kings 8:35; (7) "to be restored," Exodus 4:7; (8) "to return to God," Hosea 6:1.[28] An additional word is translated "conversion" in the Old Testament as well. The word *haphac* (הָפַךְ) occurs once, in Isaiah 60:5: "The abundance of the sea shall be converted unto thee." Here the word simply means "turn."

The Hebrew preserves much of the real nature of conversion as an actual turning around in one's way especially in the social and political spheres.[29] Tillich points out that conversion for the Hebrew person pointed to a turning around, a reversal *from* to a turning *to* something. The turning might be from injustice to justice, or from inhumanity to humanity, or from idols to gods. This twofold stress in the Hebrew is important in understanding its usage.[30] For the Hebrew, conversion was never just the experience of changing, but included a goal of action on the part of the believer where the conception of God's will was being fulfilled in turning around. It was movement back to knowing God. This movement had religious implications and was true religious conversion.

In the New Testament scriptures are recorded many instances of change from one way of life to another. The disciples were called to follow Jesus; those who met Jesus of Nazareth were healed in spirit and called to follow a new way of life. The three thousand at Pentecost, the Greeks at Antioch, the Ethiopian Eunuch, the jailer, Lydia, Paul, and Barnabas—all were called to follow. In these stories as recorded in the New Testament a change from Judaism to Christianity is implied and a movement toward God is illustrated.

Religious conversion in the New Testament is from the Hebrew *shub* (שׁוּב) and is translated by the Greek word *epistrephein* (ἐπιστρέφειν), a word used in the New Testament more than thirty-five times with the sense of (1) "turning around," Luke 1:16, 17; James speaks of the duty and privilege of bringing back, or turning back to someone who has strayed away from God, James 5:19, 20; in the "physical sense of turning or returning," Matthew 12:44, Luke 2:39, Matthew 24:18, Mark 13:16, Matthew 10:3, Luke 8:55, Luke 17:31, II Peter 2:22, and others. (2) It is used as a person turning around (Mark 5:30, Mark 8:33), but most frequently it is used to denote a mental or a spiritual turn such as in Acts 3:19, "Repent ye therefore, and be converted, that your sins may be blotted out, when the times of refreshing shall come from the presence of the Lord."[31]

Epistrephein (ἐπιστρέφειν) in classical and secular Greek reflects no experiential religious sense at all. It means to turn one's back upon someone. It is found as a Hebraism in the sense of returning to do something again or to turn the mind or the attention to someone or something. William Barclay suggests that in secular Greek more meanings for conversion are asserted: "To turn the attention of a person to someone or to something can be to warn him, to correct him to cause him to repent, and hence to convert him; and to have the attention so turned is to heed to repent, to take warning, and so to be converted."[32]

A closely related word used in the New Testament is *strephein* (στρέφειν) maning (1) "to return something to someone," Matthew 5:39; (2) "to change something into something," to bring back, return *ti* (τι) something, Matthew 27:3; (3) "turn away" as God turning away from them, Acts 7:42; (4) or "to turn, or change inwardly, or be converted," emphasizing the turning to something positive, while its opposite, "to turn to evil" would be to be "perverted."

One of the most controversial passages in scripture regarding conversion, Matthew 18:3, ("I tell you this: unless you be converted and become as little children you will not enter the kingdom of heaven") is translated in the New English Bible in its true sense as "I tell you this: unless you

turn around and become like children, you will never
enter the kingdom of heaven," indicating the relationship
of change, deep change, going to the core of the individual
for it is a turning around as well.[33]

There are instances in New Testament translations
where other Greek words have been translated "conversion." These instances involve three other Greek words
whose meaning is clear. These words are (1) *proselutos*
(προσήλυτος), a "proselyte," or a "convert" to a type of
belief, Matthew 23:15, Acts 2:10, 6:5, 13:43; (2) *aparche*
(ἀπαρχή) translated "first fruits" in the K.J.V., but modern
translators update this term to "converts," Romans 15:5, I
Corinthians 16:15; and (3) *neophutos* (νεόφυτος) translated
as "neophite." Modern translators update this word found
in I Timothy 3:6 to "recent converts." The meanings of
these related words are clear—a person newly changed in
beliefs, attitudes, or life style.

Another closely related term sometimes translated by
more modern biblical translators is the Greek term
metanoia (μετάνοια), "a change of mind."[34] *Metanoia*
(μετάνοια) seems to have several connotations of conversion including a change of mind after reflection; a going
beyond the present attitude, status, or outlook; or repen-
tance, which is also its translation. Karl Barth made a distinction between *shub* (שׁוּב) as a once and for all or repeated individual movement, and *metanoia* (μετάνοια) as
an inclusive movement in which "man moves forward
steadily to continually new things."[35] It can perhaps be
implied that the Hebrew and Greek understanding of this
movement are denoting a far more profound reorganization of man to reality than is usually meant in the popular
usage of the term conversion. Erick Routley in his book
Religious Conversion states that the word does not inevitably
imply a turning for the first time, still less "a turning for

the first and only time. It means simply stopping, turning, attending, and pursuing the new course."[36] Other words in the Latin, for example, are reflections of these basic comments, meaning again to "turn around."[37]

It seems that the primary biblical viewpoint regarding a definition of religious conversion is that it means a change, a turning around from and to a viewpoint, or a return to the principles of God. Conversion is a thorough-going turn-around, with a reorientation to the reality of life. Since the early church spoke in symbols to portray the realities of God, conversion it seems was the symbol used for the transformation. It takes on no special mystical or emotional tone in biblical usage but becomes the phrase used to describe the shift of allegiance and new direction for life. The New Testament is full of other symbols of this type to describe the shift of attention, direction, and change people of God are to experience. Followers are called out of the darkness into the light; they are to be born anew and are told to take off the old nature and put on the new. They are challenged to cultivate faith like children and enter into the kingdom of God. When they enter the relationship with God so defined, they are new creations and experience freedom. Conversion is used biblically to emphasize the same thing, an entering into a new way, in contrast to the old; a turning around in a mental sense or the more literally used physical sense. It is interesting to note that religious conversion so mentioned in the Bible does not include an analysis of the experience. In those passages where the word is used there is no connotation of an emotional upheaval or pathological break from reality that many psychologists have suggested.

The process in the Bible is considered to be supernatural and, therefore, God sent, yet man centered. Any individual who participates in the event of Jesus Christ will have a new existence, enabling him in all those areas that constitute him a person. It is obviously a mystical kind of union—one that skirts definition, but one that the Bible suggests has no specific emotional overtones. This perhaps is why it can often be spoken of as gradual as well as instantaneous. The results are the evidence. A person has been changed, and is changed, and stands changed before God. His status of condemnation is no longer valid; he stands rejoicing with Jesus Christ in victory over sin. Having personally experienced an encounter with the holy, it makes his life different from that point on.

HISTORICAL MODELS

We shall review from a historical perspective the various psychological definitions of religious conversion with the hope of establishing some commonalities for an understanding of this experience. It is to be noted here that no attempt to examine the dynamics involved is here presented; this will be discussed in the following chapter entitled "Wholeness: the Constructs of Change." There will, however, be allusions to the dynamics where the definitions of conversion touch them. This analysis of definitions will also serve as a summary of the literature available on conversion.

Early studies of religious conversion had their beginnings with G. Stanley Hall. As early as 1881 he shocked a Boston audience by suggesting that adolescence was the typical age for conversion.[38] His basic definition stated that conversion was a fundamental redirection of life, a process necessary to maturity and growing out of earlier stages of development. That redirection involved basic changes from egoism to altruism, from a pantheism to a transcendence, and in these changes each individual recapitulates the history of the race in its advance from animism to ethical lives. This definition draws heavily upon Hall's basic concepts of genetic psychology. And, "In its most fundamental sense, conversion is a natural, normal, universal, and necessary process at the stage when life pivots over from the autocentric to an heterocentric basis."[39]

Along with Hall was Edwin D. Starbuck, whose studies published in his *Psychology of Religion* proved to be monumental to the establishing of interest in the psychology of religious phenomenon.[40] In order to gather information about religious conversion he wrote to many people prominent in the religious field and asked them about their experiences. Some told of an overwhelming experience at revival meetings, in fields, jails, or bars, leaving each a changed man. Starbuck defines conversion by its *cause* rather than specifically delineating the experience. Conversion is "a process of struggling away from sin rather than of striving towards righteousness."[41] It is primarily an "un-selfing."[42] He stressed the suddenness of the experience in his definitions as well, by characterizing it as more or less sudden changes of character from evil to goodness, from sinfulness to righteousness, and from indifference to spiritual insight and activity.[43] Thus for Starbuck religious conversion was a growth process, and he wished to study all of the psychological manifestations which preceded, accompanied, and followed this experience. His definitions of conversion, however, reflected a new typology that was to form a basis for other studies on conversion. He found conversion to be of two types: (1) volitional, which he described as a spontaneous awakening and sense of the divine, and also an (2) intermediate form described as self-surrender. This insight was new and aroused much new questioning regarding conversion.[44]

A major contributor to an understanding of conversion

experience was William James. It has been suggested that James could theorize and systematize with the best of researchers, but on the whole his temperament led him to be more of an expander than an innovator. He not only looked around on those who were gaining on him but warmly welcomed each one. His interests led him to consort with mediums and to sniff nitrous oxide.[45] James has been criticized for the lack of statistics in his study on the *Varieties of Religious Experience,* originally given as the substance of the "Gifford Lectures" at the University of Edinburgh at the turn of the century. His work is based upon case studies and he allows, as much as possible, the individual to tell his own story. In *Varieties* James selected for study extreme and highly individualized forms of religious life. This represented his feeling that religion is basically an individual rather than a social phenomenon and his conviction that religion shows itself more clearly in extremes.[46] The pragmatism of William James shows through his work, for he is not as concerned in the origin of a religious experience (which may be rank superstition or pure madness for all he cares), but rather his concern is in its results. Therefore, though he is interested in the process of religious conversion, it is the usefulness and value of conversion to the individual and to those he lives with in society that make it worthwhile.[47] W. H. Clark's comments about James are relevant here:

> He insists that it is neither the origins nor the processes of the religious life that justify it so much as the results. No matter how disreputable the genesis of a religious impulse or how psychopathic the founders of a religious movement, if the consequent religious activities are beneficial to the individual or to society the religion is thereby justified.[48]

James' contributions center in four areas: (1) his emphasis on the role of experience and its results; (2) a unique concern for the individual in religion; (3) the use in mass of individual cases for the study of experiences; and (4) a respect for the role of the unconscious.[49] With these emphases James defines conversion experience through numerous case examples and declares,

> To be converted, to be regenerated, to receive grace, to experience religion, to gain assurance, are so many phrases which denote the process, gradual or sudden, by which a self hitherto divided, and consciously wrong inferior and unhappy, becomes unified and consciously right superior and happy, in consequence of its firmer hold upon religious realities. This at least is what conversion signifies in general terms, whether or not we believe that a direct divine operation is needed to bring such a moral change about.[50]

He places stress in the suddenness and crisis effect of religious conversion as well.

> Now there may be great oscillation in the emotional interest, and the hot places may shift before one almost as rapidly as the sparks that run through burnt-up paper. Then we have the wavering and divided self we heard so much of in the previous lecture. Or focus of excitement and heat, the point of view from which the aim is taken, may come to lie permanently within a certain system; and then, if the change be a religious one, we call it a *conversion*, especially if it be by crisis, or sudden.[51]

It is interesting to note that James considers change to be just change, but when given a religious terminology it becomes religious conversion.

James further defines conversion by saying "to say that a man is 'converted' means, in these terms, that religious ideas, previously peripheral in his consciousness, now take a central place, and that religious aims form the habitual center of his energy."[52] In James' definition, religious con-

version becomes a unifying experience, and his definition
centers in on an understanding of the *nature* of the experience and a dichotomy between sudden and gradual concerns, between conscious or voluntary types and involun-
tary or unconscious types.[53] In defining conversion using
this type of description, he advocates that the sudden and
gradual changes are not basically different experiences
and are both conversion. Yet as he goes on to work within this framework of experience, his own analysis does
not conform to his own definition. It is well said by Earl
Furgeson:

> By describing the gradual process as common and "less in-
> teresting" he implies that psychodynamically there is a dif-
> ference.... If James had affirmed only two ways by which
> changes in personality come about, one by gradual process of
> growth and the other by the sudden more agonizing process
> of conversion, he would have been on safe psychological
> ground, but when he identified the two as not being radically
> different he introduced a fault into the definition which his
> own analysis will not support and which the subsequent con-
> fusion will not sustain.[54]

James' definition therefore stresses unification of the
self and is defined by the *nature* of the experience and the
causes of it.[55]

George Albert Coe, early religious educator and
theorist, contributed uniquely at this time, around the
1900s, by adding an interesting insight to the definition.
Coe reacted somewhat against the contemporary emphasis
of conversion—that it was sudden and crisis-oriented. His
stress was on the religious nurture of youth, and he added
that if individuals who worked with youth especially would
play down the conflict nature, the storm and stress of religious decision, and concentrate on the normal nurture of

youth, they would have a more normal and fruitful type of religious development.[56]

George Coe saw then six senses in religious conversion that aid in its definition: (1) Conversion is a voluntary turning about or change of attitude. This sense reflects the biblical understanding of conversion. (2) It may be defined as the renunciation of one's religion and the beginning to follow another kind, or similarly a change of one branch of religious belief to another. (3) It is the means of individual salvation according to the evangelical "plan of salvation." (4) It is becoming consciously or voluntarily religious as distinguished from merely conforming to the religious mores of the family. (5) It is a quality of life of the Christian ("he is converted," etc.). (6) It is any abrupt transfer, particularly a rapid transfer, from one standpoint to another. This transformation is usually from one form of living to a higher one in an ethical sense.[57] His definition is fairly complete in that it provides various definitions to cover the myriad aspects of religious change.

George Jackson in the "Cole Lectures" for 1908, given before Vanderbilt University in the area of the psychology of conversion and later published in his book, *The Fact of Conversion*, defines religious conversion rather vaguely and reflects the mystique surrounding the fact itself. He says, "For one man conversion means the slaying of the beast within him; in another it brings the calm of conviction to an inquiet mind; for a third it is the entrance into a larger liberty and a more abundant life; and yet again it is the gathering into one the forces of the soul at war within itself."[58] A contemporary of Jackson, Harold Begbie defines conversion as a "revolution in character." He stresses "turn around" rather than the suddenness and traumatic nature of the change.[59]

All in all the early work on religious conversion, relying

heavily upon questionnaire and case study information, established conversion as a fact of the Christian life. This fact reflected the historical times as well, for conversion was an actual form of entry into the Christian life stemming from the early revivals in the eighteenth and nineteenth centuries. William James, quoting the New England Puritan Joseph Alleine, points to the symbolic nature of conversion by saying it is "not the putting in a patch of holiness; but with the true convert holiness is woven into all his powers, principles, and practice. The sincere Christian is quite a new fabric, from the foundation to the top-stone. He is a new man, a new creature."[60] Conversion was considered a depth change, characterized by typologies that included those defined by nature (sudden or gradual) and those defined by cause (volitional or self-surrender).

In 1910 the *Psychology of Religious Experience* was published by E. S. Ames. His viewpoint was that religion has its origin in the attempt to conserve social value. Ames agrees with Begbie in his definition in defining religious conversion as only a sudden, intense, and extreme emotional experience.[61] James H. Leuba, a teacher at Bryn Mawr College, began to publish during this same period. Leuba differed in his approach to the psychology of religion and tended toward more naturalistic explanations of religious phenomena, pointing out, for example, the similarity of the reports of mystics to those of people who have been under the influence of drugs.[62] Yet he defined religious conversion by its *causes* rather than directly defining it. He understood religious conversion to be the result of the conflict within people and believed it to be a method of seeking "wholeness" within a person. He is one of the first to assume the integrating force within conversion for personality.[63]

In 1913, Robert Thouless defined religious conversion

on the basis of *content* rather than nature or cause. He defines conversion as a process with contents primarily intellectual, moral, or social. He states:

> Religious conversion is the name commonly given to the process which leads to the adoption of a religious attitude; the process may be gradual or sudden. It is likely to include a change in belief on religious topics, but this will be accompanied by changes in the motivation to behavior and in reactions to the social environment. One or another of these directions of change may seem to play the predominant role in the conversion change. One may then speak of intellectual, or moral, or social conversions. The distinctions between them are not, however, clear cut; every intellectual change has its implications for behavior and for social allegiances, and no one is likely to change his social allegiance in religion or his behavior motivation without some corresponding change in what he believes.[64]

In illustrating these types he suggests that of all the three kinds of conversion, Paul's would be of the social variety. Paul's change seems to have been from one system of loyalties to another, and he claims that there is no evidence that the conflict was one between opposing opinions, nor was the change from a wrong to a right system. Rather, Paul's change was from two systems equally right at the time for Paul.[65] This question could be debated, however, for Paul's conversion was to a new way of life, one that condemned the previous way as being wrong. Therefore, there would have to be moral tones within the conversion, especially if one is to define conversion according to content.

An illustration of moral conversion is that of one "swearing Tom," whose conflict was a primarily moral one and the change to be adopted was from an old way of life, one of swearing, to a new way where the old life style was ruled out.[66]

Finding examples of religious conversion defined by its intellectual elements is much more difficult, according to Thouless. A choice between two systems of thought where the decision is between the one that is true and the one claimed false is rare indeed. Thouless states that they may even be found only in the annals of literature, and quotes two examples of this type, Mrs. Ward's novel, *Robert Ellsmere,* and Masefield's *The Everlasting Mercy.* These are examples of changes from Christianity to agnosticism and from agnosticism to Christianity, respectively.[67] An interesting historical commentary on evangelistic technique is given by Thouless as a reason for so few documented intellectual conversions.

> A purely intellectual conversion, uncomplicated by elements of moral or social conflict, is perhaps not to be found in real life. Certainly one will not find them in the records of evangelists since these do not commonly argue with individual members of their audiences and generally doubt the value of an intellectual appeal. Yet there are cases of individuals whose main problem has been that of accepting as true the propositions of religion and whose central change has been the acceptance of a system of beliefs that was previously held to be false. No doubt, other factors come into such a person's conversion; he must change his behavior motivation and loyalties too, but the belief may seem to him to be the primary thing from which these others follow.[68]

In the 1920s there appeared a book which perhaps is second only to James's *Varieties of Religious Experience* in the field of the psychology of religion. This was James B. Pratt's *The Religious Consciousness.* James Pratt was a graduate of Williams College and spent most of his life teaching at his *alma mater.* He had done some work in the field while a graduate student at Harvard and had published earlier in 1907 in this area as well. He was a member of the gradualist school of thought regarding religious conversion and claims that religious conversion is "a gradual and almost imperceptible process." Little consideration is given for the "sudden" typology of James or Ames, but he spends some time defending the idea that all change is gradual, even Paul's perhaps.[69]

John Oman at the same time suggests that conversion is not a subconscious change of nature, but is itself a "conscious discernment of our true relation to God and man."[70] His emphasis on the centrality of personal awareness in the conversion process reflects James' concern for individuality in these kinds of experiences. Integral to the sense of awareness of the process is a conscious decision in which the reality of "ultimate Being is acknowledged, confessed, apprehended, returned to."[71]

By the 1920s there was a more generalized acceptance of the concepts of psychoanalysis. Sigmund Freud himself dealt with religious conversion only briefly in a short paper in 1927. A young physician had written to Freud about a religious experience of his that had happened shortly after he had seen an old woman on a dissecting table. Because of this the young man was temporarily thrown into a religious disbelief, conflict, then strong belief. He is analyzed as undergoing a stimulated Oedipal jealousy and anger which had been directed at the father for the sadistic, sexualized degradation of the mother, which was represented by the old woman. Freud theorized that because the man's understanding of God and Father were basically interrelated, the anger and rebellion that was experienced were expressed in atheistic form. But for fear of the omnipotence of God he was forced to a sudden return to faith, which was experienced as a moment called conversion.[72] Religious conversion is here defined as a reaction process and defined by its cause again.

During the 1920s Oskar Pfister wrote about the apostle Paul's conversion. Through a detailed reconstruction of Paul's life, most notably his childhood, he arrived at some interesting conclusions. He labeled Paul a "hysteric" dealing with unconscious sexual guilt. And thus religious conversion was defined again by *cause*.[73] Those of this school of thought, like Pfister, tend to classify conversion experience as a phenomenon of psychopathology. Surely some religious conversion experiences find their source in pathology, yet this definition alone does not seem to be broad enough to fit what is generally considered conversion, nor validate the totality of research.[74]

Henry Nelson Wieman uses the word "unification" to define religious conversion and stresses a sort of fusion that makes man whole; "it means that he is made whole . . . fused into a single total system in which each element sustains every other."[75] This reflects later concerns of Gordon Allport and Leslie Weatherhead as they discuss conversion as an integration or reintegration process.[76] This aspect of wholeness and unification is an essential element in defining religious conversion, I believe, for its role in identity formation may reflect this sense of wholeness and unification of reality into more meaningful concepts.

In 1927 a volume that dealt with the typical experiences of those converted to Catholicism was released by Sante de Sanctis. He saw conversion only to be a gradual process, as the end result of a lifelong development.[77] Being a gradualist in this manner allowed him to define conversion by nature rather than cause, yet his rather one-sided definition allowed the developmental process of growth to be emphasized. Since religious beliefs and ideas typically begin within childhood, equating conversion with growth was natural. Since religious conversion is gradual, and is usually preceded by antecedent experiences and conditions, then it is like growth in its occurrence; they therefore must be alike. This is the logical outcome of illogical reasoning, for its empties conversion of its dynamics and tends to make the experience so vague as to generalize a specific experience away. His definition reads: "The crisis conversion . . . need, therefore, be nothing but an episode in a slow psychic process. . . ."[78] The fact that his studies were on change of experience within the Catholic community may have tempered his decision since crisis, sudden experiences, or experiences that, though gradual, had a decisive act of decision involved in them, were seldom experienced in his audience.

Elmer T. Clark proposed during this time that religious conversion be defined solely as a more radical and emotional change from irreligion to religion and adds the term "religious awakening" to describe the entry into a religious experience.[79] His study was one of the largest ever done in this field as he examined a large company which included some 985 Methodists, 366 Presbyterians, 252 Baptists, and 133 members of the confirmation group of churches. He is criticized because his study portrayed a cross section during a religious period when conversion had gone out of style as a way of entry into faith and he could be expected to report only in the terms he did.[80] He is also criticized in that his subjects were practically all middle-class college students and therefore not typical of the population of the day. Of this population only a small proportion reported sudden religious conversions.[81]

By the 1930s, understanding of behavior in terms of adaptation began to be a common viewpoint and the definitions of religious conversions reflect this viewpoint. Up to this time most defining conversion made use of descriptions which incorporated either a sudden or gradual dichotomy, or looked to its contents to classify it; more were now beginning to signify conversion by its *cause*. W. Lawson Jones, a British psychologist, formulated religious conversion as part of a general adaptational process dealing with the whole of an individual's life situation. He included both intrapsychic and environmental conflict resolution as its cause.[82] A most intriguing definition of conversion, almost secular, was also presented in the 1930s by L. W. Grensted, who stated that religious conversion is simply the building up a sense of wholeness of being. This stress on the *function* of conversion in its definition became a new trend. His conviction that the central issue in conversion was wholeness allowed him to see man as a total unit and to see conversion as a positive aid in the unity of man. His definition was very broad. He would even include any change in any sphere that tended toward wholeness as conversion, but classified those changes in a religious setting as holiness or sanctity, "the outcome of the process of sanctification."[83]

Another definition at this period of history was Mary Ewer's three understandings of this process: (1) the gradual transmutation of the nature itself; (2) a conscious, usually catastrophic, "new birth" into a filial relationship with God; and (3) a turning point or change of direction.[84] This simplistic concept brings all concerns about religious conversion to the front.

From a context of mental illness, both personal and theoretical, Anton T. Boisen formulated in 1936 a theory of conversion as an alternative to schizophrenia or schizoid states in the resolution of personal problems. When he added his author's note to the 1952 edition of his book, *The Exploration of the Inner World,* he resubstantiated his earlier viewpoint that religious conversion is the more or less sudden change of character from sinfulness to righ-

teousness or from indifference to spiritual awakening aris-
ing out of the problem-solving of mental tasks. He states:

> ... Both may arise out of a common situation—that of inner
> conflict and disharmony, accompanied by a keen awareness of
> ultimate loyalties and unattained possibilities. Religious ex-
> perience as well as mental disorder may involve severe emo-
> tional upheaval and mental disorder as well as religious ex-
> perience may represent the operation of the healing forces of
> nature. The conclusion follows that certain types of mental
> disorder and certain types of religious experience are alike
> attempts at reorganization. The difference lies in the out-
> come. Where the attempt is successful and some degree of
> victory is won, it is commonly recognized as religious experi-
> ence. Where it is unsuccessful or indeterminate, it is com-
> monly spoken of as "insanity."[85]

With this viewpoint, some types of honest, desperate
mental illness are literally the same as this sudden eruptive
kind of conversion. For Boisen, the event of religious conversion as abrupt and eruptive serves to bring the cause of
distress from the realm of evasion and concealment out
into the realm of clear awareness. "Such disturbances
often serve as a sort of judgment day, the patient blurting
out what before, for the life of him, he would not have
dared to say."[86] Religious conversion is then defined as an
attempt at repair or elimination and is experienced as a
reorganization of his entire mental structure and a revalu-
ation of values. Boisen refers to Starbuck's concepts as he
equates his understanding with them.

> It is important to bear in mind that such acute disturbances
> are closely related to the religious conversion experience.
> ... According to Starbuck's findings such conversion ex-
> periences are likewise an eruptive breaking up of evil habits
> and abnormal tastes and the turning of vital forces along new
> channels. In mental disorder of this type we therefore have a

manifestation of the power that makes for health just as truly as we do in the religious conversion experience.[87]

Leon Salzman makes one of the first contributions in trying to understand religious conversion in terms of its *dynamics*. Linking religious conversion with any change accomplished at a given time, he stresses the suddenness of the experience and defines it in terms of its *psychodynamics*, or, as he says, it is "Any change of religion or of moral, political, ethical, or esthetic views which occur in the life of a person either with or without a mystical experience, and which is motivated by strong pressures within the person."[88] In every case of conversion, religious or non-religious, he recognizes an incubation period and a precipitating event and therefore labels two types of conversion according to result: (1) the progressive or maturational kind, and (2) the regressive or psychopathological kind.[89]

> Religious conversion is a specific instance of the general principle of change in the process of human adaptation. Conversion is a generic term for change and generally implies a drastic alteration of a former state . . . in theological terms it has been used in a special sense to imply a marked alteration of one's spiritual state through a superior power, generally meaning a Godhead.[90]

His insight in allowing conversion to be through natural factors proves most helpful in understanding it. His addendum regarding those changes that are caused by pressing personal and interpersonal difficulties which have no spiritual significance, yet may be dressed in religious language or symbolism, gives a broader understanding to the process of human change.[91] This does not deny that God, or Being, is in some way active in these natural changes; it only opens the person to find some actual cause for the change. If the change is beneficial, then it serves its purpose in integrating the life. In my own opinion, if a knowledge of Diety and man's relationship to others is enhanced, the experience will be actualizing in the life of the believer, growth will take place, and religious identity will be established, an important factor in identity formation which will be discussed later.

Two others in this period that have proposed definitions are Owen Brandon and Pitirim Sorokin. Owen Brandon seems unsatisfied to rely upon defining conversion as gradual or sudden change, but amplifies these two kinds of religious conversion to include some four or five others, each gradations of the two basic, usual types.[92] Sorokin isolates factors in any conversion experience itself rather than to define it, seeing identification with a supreme value rearrangement of ego and values and group affiliation the criteria for defining conversion.[93]

CONTEMPORARY MODELS

One of the most interesting contributions to the field of religious conversion experience has been William Sargent's additions to the field of study. His *Battle for the Mind* correlates conversion with Chinese brain-washing and thought-reform techniques. He defines religious conversion by *function*. Conversion for Sargent becomes a process akin to self-abnegation and brain-washing. He traces the long history of the many uses of psychological conditioning through the generation of intense anxiety or strong emotion, such as fear, hate, guilt, anger, which are used to wipe the cortical slate clean and thus disorganize the individual so new patterns of belief and action can be established. These new ways are usually induced by suggestion

and approved by the one who suggests them.[94] His definition points up the relationship of suggestion to conversion
process and gives an important insight into the way the
mind functions in causing changes. Yet he attributes conversion to a normal brain process and stresses the *cause,*
being suggestion, and *function,* being reorganization, in
defining it.

Orlo Strunk, Jr., writing about the psychology of religion, includes a major emphasis regarding religious conversion. His position includes in his definition a modern
aspect of psychology. He suggests that the process active in
conversion is a "binding" which is perhaps conversion's
fundamental dynamic and leads to an organization and
completion of man's various dimensions. Strunk equates
the religious conversion experience with that of "actualiza-
tion," that process which helps to stabilize, interiorize, and
motivate man. Conversion is defined by *effect* then and is
the process in which man realizes himself.[95]

In the 1960s Carl Christensen, a psychiatrist, made
perhaps one of the most complete contributions to the
long list of those who concerned themselves with religious
conversion. His 1963 paper, "Religious Conversion," reported on some twenty-two patients of his who had experienced religious conversions during adolescence. In
each of the reported cases, these people suffered unusual
conflict in their early lives and, according to Christensen,
significant ego impairment.[96] The people studied also had
rigid church backgrounds, which he theorized originally
served as a haven for acceptance but later became their
source for anxiety and guilt. It was at this time that extreme hallucinatory conversions occurred.[97] Christensen is
unique among writers on conversion in that he is quick to
inform those interested in his work that he has a rather
narrowly-defined area in which he works when discussing

conversion. Conversion then for Christensen is defined as "an acute hallucinatory episode occurring within the framework of religious belief and characterized by its subjective intensity, apparent suddenness of onset, brief duration, auditory, and sometimes visual hallucinations, and an observable change in the subsequent behavior of the convert."[98]

Since Christensen is mostly concerned with conversion as an adolescent experience, he stresses the suddenness of it and suggests that conversion does not include other forms of religious experience, which while they may eventually have a similar result, lack the acute reactions.[99]

Other more contemporary contributors to the literature of conversion include William Barclay, who sees religious conversion in the biblical sense as a "change" and considers "the most serious mistake . . . is to standardize the experience of conversion, and to (invite) the inevitable result . . . that the normal conversion experience must be sudden, shattering, and complete . . . there will be no one standardized conversion experience; but the experience of conversion will be an infinitely varied as human experience itself."[100]

W. S. Hill sees religious conversion defined by its *depth*, not its speed,[101] while John E. Smith suggests that conversion can be categorized, for it may be total transformation, it may be an alteration in some identifiable feature of a person's life and experience, or "it may be thought of as a more radical transformation involving a change of total personality."[102]

Seward Hiltner, a theologian, presents a variation to the usual definition of religious conversion when he suggests that it is to be defined as a "movement" rather than a "once-for-all completed fact." Secondly, it is to be considered a common compelling growth experience to those in their thirties rather than as just an adolescent experience; it is as well a function of the church through education and pastoral care, and is truly to be defined as the decisive joining of a fellowship to those who, "though sinners, yet saved, reach out in evangelism, in missions, and in social service and reform to share the treasure that God's grace in Jesus Christ has brought to them."[103] His definition is obviously limited to a function of mission of the church; even though this type of conversion experience may be considered a valid function of the church, it negates the vast amount of evidence that it is more. Hiltner's "conversion" is only one kind and his definition is too narrow to provide a good, meaningful description to those who seek to understand the experience.

Those that do not provide a definition of their concepts of religious conversion include Joel Allison, who suggests that its cause is a regression in the service of the ego and very well may be a positive activity.[104] Some contemporary writers, such as Charles Stewart, define religious conversion very specifically as "the change from egocentricity to concern for other persons, from separation from persons to reconciliation with them, or from isolation to community may occur in the adolescent by a sudden overturn of his emotions and by emergence of a new and different orientation."[105] William Silverberg calls it the "schizoid maneuver," yet Stewart deals with a concern for adolescence and his definition reflects this. Stewart's definition is based on social distinctions, thus adding another dimension to the definition.

W. H. Clark, psychologist of religion, more recently has suggested that conversion should be defined as a sharp and sudden break with a person's "past ideas, attitudes, values, or behavior, more generally all four of these, accompanied by intense feeling. . . . It is always recognized by the participants as religious."[106] Clark reflects earlier concerns with the nature of the experience and deals as well with religious conversion as being gradual, which contradicts his first definition. He suggests that most sudden conversions have their gradual elements.[107] James Dittes defines it like the broad concept—religion. Conversion may represent primarily a change of institutional allegiance or may take place within highly emotional frameworks, or may occur when it is the generally prescribed form which is normative within the group. Or "conversion may simply refer to a much more subjective and private change of orientation and values."[108]

Other individuals could be cited, for almost everyone who has written about religious experience attempts some type of definition of religious conversion. Whether a gradual change, a sudden emotional experience, a changing of allegiance, or a turning from self to others or God, conversion is a vital force in the life. It plays a significant role in the construction of identity, pointing a life in a particular direction, giving it an aim. To determine the way conversion performs these functions, it will be necessary to examine the constituent elements of the phenomena.

NOTES

1. John 3:3, King James Version.
2. H. R. Bagwell, "Abrupt Religious Conversion Experience," *Journal of Religion and Health,* VIII (April, 1969), p. 174.
3. J. R. Scroggs and W. G. T. Douglas, "Issues in the Psychology of Religious Conversion," *Journal of Religion and Health,* VI (July, 1967), p. 204.
4. William James, *The Varieties of Religious Experience,* Mentor

Books (New York: New American Library of World Literature, Inc., 1958), p. 184.

5. John Wesley, *The Journal of John Wesley,* ed. by Nehemiah Curnock (London: Epworth Press, 1938), pp. 186–204.

6. Augustine, *The Confessions of St. Augustine,* trans. by Rex Warner, Mentor-Omega Books (New York: New American Library of World Literature, Inc., 1963), p. 183.

7. From *Pensees,* quoted in Robert H. Thouless, *An Introduction to the Psychology of Religion* (Cambridge: Cambridge University Press, 1971), p. 117.

8. Ibid., p. 116.

9. W. S. Hill, "Psychology of Conversion," *Pastoral Psychology,* VI (November, 1955), p. 44.

10. Barbara Eleanor Jones, "Conversion: An Examination of the Myth of Human Change" (unpublished Ph.D. dissertation, Columbia University, 1969), p. 4.

11. Paul Tillich, *The Protestant Era* (Chicago: University of Chicago Press, 1948), pp. xv, 58, 87, 273.

12. John H. Westerhoff III, *Generation to Generation* (Philadelphia: United Church Press, 1974).

13. Walter Houston Clark, *The Psychology of Religion* (New York: Macmillan Co., 1958), p. 22.

14. Ruth Ann Wallace, "Some Social Determinants of Change of Religious Affiliation" (unpublished Ph.D. dissertation, University of California at Berkeley, 1968), p. 13.

15. Paul Tillich, *Systematic Theology,* (3 vols.; Chicago: University of Chicago Press, 1951–63), III, p. 221.

16. John Dewey, *A Common Faith* (New Haven: Yale University Press, 1940), p. 10.

17. Romans 8:38–39, Revised Standard Version.

18. Leon Salzman, "The Psychology of Religions and Ideological Conversion," *Psychiatry,* XVI 1953, p. 117.

19. "Conversion," *Webster's New Twentieth Century Dictionary: Unabridged* (2nd ed., 1959), p. 400.

20. John E. Smith, "The Concept of Conversion," *Mid-Stream,* VIII, No. 3 (1966), p. 14.

21. Michael Argyle, *Religious Behavior* (London: Routledge, 1958).

22. John Baillie, *Baptism and Conversion* (New York: Charles Scribner's Sons, 1963), p. 51.

23. George Barton Cutten, *The Psychological Phenomena of Christianity* (New York: Charles Scribner's Sons, 1908), p. 234.

24. Elmer T. Clark, *The Psychology of Religious Awakening* (New York: Macmillan Co., 1929), p. 36.

25. The Revised Standard Version's rendition of this passage translates *shub* (שׁוּב) as "reviving the soul."

26. The New English Version here translates *shub* (שׁוּב) "repentant."

27. Robert Baker Girdlestone, *Synonyms of the Old Testament* (Grand Rapids, Mich.: Wm. B. Eerdmans Publishing Co., 1897), p. 92.

28. William Barclay, *Turning to God* (London: The Epworth Press, 1963), p. 24.

29. Bernhard Citron, *New Birth: A Study of the Evangelical Doctrine of Conversion in the Protestant Fathers* (Edinburgh: University Press, 1951), p. 14.

30. Tillich, *Systematic Theology*, p. 218.

31. The New English Bible has this text translated, "Repent then and turn to God, so that your sins may be wiped out." This implies a turning *from* something again and a return *to* God.

32. Barclay, *Turning to God*, pp. 18, 19.

33. William Barclay (*Turning to God*, p. 22) suggests for the text in Matthew 18:3 the following interesting comment in explanation. "In this passage the word which is translated converted is exactly the same word and the same tense of the word which is used of Jesus turning around. In the passages in which it is used of Jesus, it is the aorist particle *strapheis* (στραφείς) which is used. Here it is the aorist tense *straphete* (στραφῆτε). When *strephein* (στρέφειν) is so used for turning it is middle; that is to say, the verb is passive in form, but active in meaning, as with deponent verbs in Latin, it is therefore quite clear that in the Matthew passage the translation should be active and not passive. It ought to be, not 'except ye be converted,' but unless you turn, unless you change. Both the word convert and the passive use of the word introduce wrong overtones into the translation. It is not technical conversions which is here being spoken of; it is a turning of the mind so that man's outlook on, and attitude to, life are altered from pride to humility."

34. William Arndt and F. Wilbur Gingrich, *A Greek-English*

Lexicon of the New Testament and Other Early Christian Literature (Chicago: University of Chicago Press, 1957), p. 778.

35. Karl Barth, *Church Dogmatics,* trans. by G. W. Bromiley, et al. (4 vols. Edinburgh: T. and T. Clark, 1936–1962), IV, p. 567.

36. Erick Routley, *Religious Conversion,* trans. by Helen Augur (New York: Harcourt, Brace, 1927), p. 31.

37. Theologian Seward Hiltner ("Toward a Theology of Conversion in the Light of Psychology," *Pastoral Psychology,* XVII (1966), pp. 35–42) suggests this interesting discussion with himself as he discovered the Latin usage of this term. "Recently I got out my Latin dictionary and looked up *converto.* I was not surprised to find 'turn around,' even though I got a slight jar from the synonym, 'whirl around.' In Cicero, I found, it meant 'to turn in the opposite direction,' which is not so surprising if you get a proper definition of what 'opposite' means. But I was truly startled to find the *conversio* meant, in Cicero, 'a periodical return.' No one and for allness here! And I was even more astonished to think of the relationship between *conversio* and *conversatio,* the root of our modern 'conversation,' which routinely meant 'frequent use,' but which in Seneca, meant 'dealings with person'. . . Conversion it seems, is a real turning around, even in the opposite direction (if you can figure out just what opposite means). Like a weather vane, it may be periodic; and, like the related conversation, it may have a truly social reference. . . . An alcoholic who turns around and now kisses his wife and pays the bills is equally converted."

38. Walter Houston Clark, "Intense Religious Experience," *Research on Religious Development: A Comprehensive Handbook,* ed. by M. Strommen (New York: Hawthorn Books, Inc., 1971), p. 532.

39. Robert N. Beck, "Hall's Genetic Psychology and Religious Conversion," *Pastoral Psychology,* XVI (September, 1965), p. 47.

40. Starbuck was early in the modern American movement in the study of religion and when one reads his volume, one is impressed with the tremendous time given to conversion experience. Clark (*Psychology of Religion,* p. 7) suggests that this was the fashion of the day in most Protestant evangelical circles and that the book only reflects the times. Yet his book received wide acclaim and was later translated into German.

41. E. D. Starbuck, *The Psychology of Religion* (New York: Charles Scribner's Sons, 1915), p. 64.

42. Ibid., p. 145.

43. Ibid., p. 21.

44. William Paterson, *Conversion* (New York: Charles Scribner's Sons, 1940), p. 161.

45. Walter Houston Clark, "William James: Contributions to the Psychology of Religious Conversion," *Pastoral Psychology*, XVI (September, 1965), p. 30.

46. James, *Religious Experience*, pp. 21–37; pp. 168–174; lecture XX.

47. Walter Houston Clark, "William James: Contributions to the Psychology of Religious Conversion," *Christianity Today* (May 12, 1967, 1958), pp. 5–20.

48. Clark, *The Psychology of Religion*, p. 8.

49. James, *Religious Experience*, see pp. 367–390.

50. Ibid., p. 157.

51. Ibid., p. 162.

52. Ibid., p. 162.

53. Ibid., p. 202.

54. Earl H. Furgeson, "The Definition of Religious Conversion," *Pastoral Psychology*, XVI (September, 1965), p. 9.

55. James, *Religious Experience*, p. 169.

56. George Albert Coe, *The Spiritual Life* (New York: Eaton and Mains, 1900), pp. 35–52.

57. George Albert Coe, *Psychology of Religion* (Chicago: University of Chicago Press, 1917), p. 152.

58. George Jackson, *The Fact of Conversion: The Cole Lectures for 1908* (New York: Fleming H. Revell Co., 1908), p. 97.

59. Harold Begbie, *Twice-Born Man* (New York: Fleming H. Revell Co., 1909), p. 18.

60. James, *Religious Experience*, p. 185.

61. Ed S. Ames, *The Psychology of Religious Experience* (Boston: Houghton-Mifflin Co., 1910), p. 251.

62. Clark, *The Psychology of Religion*, p. 9.

63. Carl W. Christensen, "Religious Conversion in Adolescence," *Pastoral Psychology*, XVI (September, 1965), p. 19.

64. Thouless, *Introduction*, p. 104.

65. Ibid., p. 105.

66. Ibid., p. 106.

67. Ibid., pp. 106-107.

68. Ibid., p. 107.

69. James Bissett Pratt, *The Religious Consciousness: A Psychological Study* (New York: Macmillan Co., 1926), p. 153.

70. John Oman, *Grace and Personality* (Cambridge: University Press, 1925).

71. Ibid.

72. Sigmund Freud, "A Religious Experience," *Sigmund Freud: Collected Papers,* ed. by James Strachey, Vol. V (New York: Basic Books, Inc., Publishers, 1959), p. 243.

73. Oskar Pfister, *"Die Entwicklung des Apostels Paulus,"* Imago, IV (1920), p. 243.

74. Carl Christensen, a physician, in "Religious Conversion in Adolescence," p. 17, suggests "since psychiatry is concerned with mental disorders, much of the psychiatric contributions to the understanding of religious belief have emphasized psychopathology. Sometimes, psychiatrists tend to forget that religion is a normal part of man's individual and cultural life." Scroggs and Douglas in "Issues," pp. 213-215, conclude that those psychologists whose commitment is to the Christian faith tend to view conversion as healthy, normal, and leading to maturity, while those who do not share this concern are most likely to see religious conversion as regressive and pathological. James avoids the issue altogether and focuses instead of fruits rather than roots.

75. Henry Nelson Wieman, *Religious Experience and Scientific Method* (New York: Macmillan Co., 1926), p. 219.

76. See Gordon Allport, *The Individual and His Religion: A Psychological Interpretation* (New York: Macmillan Co., 1950), pp. 92-95; or Leslie D. Weatherhead, *Psychology, Religion and Healing* (London: Hodder and Stoughton, Ltd., 1952), p. 467.

77. Bagwell, "Abrupt Religious Conversion Experience," p. 167.

78. Sante de Sanctis, *Religious Conversion: A Bio-Psychological Study* (London: Kegan Paul, Trench, Trubner & Co., 1927), p. 84.

79. Clark, *The Psychology of Religious Awakening*, p. 96.

80. Paterson, *Conversion,* pp. 154-155.

81. Clark, "Intense Religious Experience," p. 532.
82. H. R. Bagwell, "Abrupt Religious Conversion Experience," p. 169.
83. L. W. Grensted, *Psychology and God: A Study of the Implications of Recent Psychology for Religious Belief and Practice* (London: Longmans, Green and Co., 1930), p. 86.
84. Mary Anita Ewer, *A Survey of Mystical Symbolism* (New York: Macmillan Co., 1933), p. 197.
85. Anton T. Boisen, *The Exploration of the Inner World* (New York: Harper & Bros., 1936), p. viii.
86. Ibid., p. 196.
87. Ibid., p. 159.
88. Leon Salzman, "The Psychology of Regressive Religious Conversion," *Journal of Pastoral Care,* VIII, No. 2 (1954), p. 63.
89. Carl W. Christensen, "Religious Conversion in Adolescence," p. 20.
90. Leon Salzman, "Types of Religious Conversion," *Pastoral Psychology,* XVII (1966), p. 10.
91. Ibid.
92. Owen Brandon, *The Battle for the Soul* (Philadelphia, Penn.: Westminster Press, 1959), p. 27.
93. Pitirim A. Sorokin, *The Ways of Power and Love: Types, Factors and Techniques of Moral Transformation* (Boston, Mass.: Beacon Press, 1954), pp. 119-120, 148-154.
94. See William Sargent, *Battle for the Mind* (New York: Harper & Row, 1957) as an example.
95. Orlo Strunk, *Religion: A Psychological Interpretation* (New York: Abingdon Press, 1962), p. 74.
96. As reported by Carl W. Christensen, "Religious Conversion," *Archives of General Psychiatry,* IX (September, 1963), pp. 207-216. The patients studied were two with schizophrenia, one schizoid, and nineteen others with various neurotic tendencies.
97. Ibid.
98. Ibid., p. 207.
99. Carl W. Christensen, "Religious Conversion in Adolescence," p. 18.
100. Barclay, *Turning to God,* pp. 92-93.
101. W. S. Hill, "Psychology of Conversion," *Pastoral Psychology,* VI (November, 1955), p. 46.

102. John E. Smith, "The Concept of Conversion," Mid-Stream, VIII, No. 3 (1966), p. 16.

103. Seward Hiltner, "Toward A Theology of Conversion in the Light of Psychology," *Pastoral Psychology,* XVII (September, 1966), p. 35.

104. Joel Allison, "Recent Empirical Studies of Religious Conversion Experiences," *Pastoral Psychology,* XVII, No. 166 (September, 1966), p. 22.

105. Charles William Stewart, *Adolescent Religion: A Developmental Study of the Religion of Youth* (Nashville: Abingdon Press, 1967), p. 266.

106. Clark, "Intense Religious Experience," p. 531.

107. Ibid.

108. James E. Dittes, "Two Issues in Measuring Religion," in *Research on Religious Development: A Comprehensive Handbook,* ed. Merton P. Strommen (New York: Hawthorn Books, Inc., 1971), p. 81.

CHAPTER II

WHOLENESS: The Constructs of Change

"In the evening I went very unwillingly to a society in Aldersgate Street, where one was reading Luther's preface to the *Epistle to the Romans.* About a quarter of nine, while he was describing the change which God works in the heart through faith in Christ, I felt my heart strangely warmed. I felt I did trust in Christ alone for my salvation; and an assurance was given me that He had taken away *my* sins, *even* mine, and saved *me* from the law of sin and death." John Wesley.

When one looks over the possibilities of defining the term religious conversion, one is made aware of the many avenues available for definition. Definitions seem to stress causality when observed are such things as motives, intuition, or volition. When one attempts to analyze conversion experience itself in such terms as sudden or gradual, acute, confusional, dramatic, pathological, or positive, the definitions reflect an attempt to define its *essence* or *nature*. Those who wish to look at the *content* stress the intellectual, emotional, social, moral, philosophical, or religious elements or beliefs involved. Those who stress the *function* in the life of the individual see the binding, integrating, and bonding functionality of the experience. Those definitions of conversion that are simply symbolic tend to be too vague and therefore not very helpful; an example is de Sanctis's definition of conversion as a "displacement of psychic energy or a new economy of love."[1]

There has been a gradual shift throughout the history of studies about religious conversion in this century. Early studies of conversion simply described the process. Then as men began studying the issue afresh, most have involved themselves in the elaboration of the hypothesis that the process of religious conversion be related to general theories of personality and behavioral change. This is only logical because the new insights of psychoanalysis and psychology since Freud have centered in on the changing aspects of mankind as he lives, which would necessarily include religious expression.

One conclusion is that there are different kinds of emphases in the study of religious conversion, and a general feeling of the psychological school observes that Christianity continues to produce examples of a radical transformation of character, but that there is much greater variety than theology had recognized in the attainment, the forms, and the content of the experience.[2] One is tempted to agree with Jackson when he criticized attempts to define conversion in a limited sense by saying, "It matters . . . little what principle of classification we adopt, or whether we adopt any at all—the best is imperfect—what does matter is that we steadfastly resist all attempts to 'standardize' conversion. There are types of conversion to which many do not conform. There is none to which any must conform."[3]

It is important then to insist that there are many varieties of religious conversion experience and any definition that does not allow for the individual variations due to genetics, environment, tradition, or personality variables has negated an important fundamental point. Individuality, uniqueness, and separateness must be allowed. Since it is not the purpose to decide whether or not conversion experiences are religiously true or not, a definition that stresses *function* and *process* is perhaps the most decisive for use in this book, and the most useful in understanding the experience. Therefore it is posed that religious conversion be defined by constituent elements, those processes that are operant in the religious experience. This would then be labeled religious conversion.

It is obvious that the most consistent theme that runs throughout the research on conversion is that the experience typifies "change." The original words signify that change of a deep nature, a return to earlier allegiances, or a shifting around of attitude and belief constitute the best understanding of the word. If conversion means "change," the converted person is one who has changed his way of life. But, if conversion only means change, then obviously all types of change, good or bad, toward helpful or harmful things would as well constitute religious conversion, or as Earl Furgeson suggests, "A person who gets married has changed his way of life, but he is not usually thought of as having been converted."[4] There is with religious conversion various connotations that equally influence the definition. Most of these are the connotations of the wild emotionalist, revivalist, Bible-beating circuit preacher who scared hell-fire and damnation into those who watched. Or we think of the dramatic tongue speaker who shouts or shakes.[5]

When religious conversion experience is totally equated with change, the psychological essence of the experience itself is dissipated and made almost indistinguishable from change itself. This was the motivation for E. T. Clark in 1929 to eliminate the use and confusion of the term conversion by simply avoiding the use of the word. Attention must also be called to the fact that, as illustrated by the previous discussion of definitions of religious conversion, conversion is only a part of a total process, of which the final product is religious experience. Therefore it is suggested that for an experience of change to be religious conversion, constituent elements must be present. These elements make the essence of religious conversion, and without them the experience should not be classified as one of religious conversion. Illustration 1 on the following page shows the elements joining to define religious conversion. This will be used as a basis for reflecting upon the identity experience later. A brief discussion of each element in the definition will follow.

Religious conversion then is a word used to describe "change," but more specifically, a kind of change that has the following constituent elements: (1) a unifying quality for self, which includes self-integration, wholeness, and possible reorganization; (2) a positive resultant function; (3) intensity of commitment to an ideology, usually thought of as occurring within the Christian tradition as a confrontation with ultimates, but may include change with any subjective religious quality; (4) includes a decisive "change or returning to" brought on suddenly or gradually, seen as either instantaneous or incubational.

One reason that there is so much diversity of definition regarding religious conversion is that each views conversion from his own vantage point. If it is a theological viewpoint, then his definition might entirely eliminate the human element and speak of it in totally theological rather than psychological terms, as a divine act which changes one. Those who select a naturalistic viewpoint simply eliminate the religious connotations entirely. So it is not simply a matter of selecting the major twenty-two definitions and getting at their substance to understand religious conversion totally. The result of this type of definition would

CONSTITUENT ELEMENTS OF CONVERSION

Illustration 1: Conversion is a word used to describe "change," but a kind of change that includes the following constituent elements.

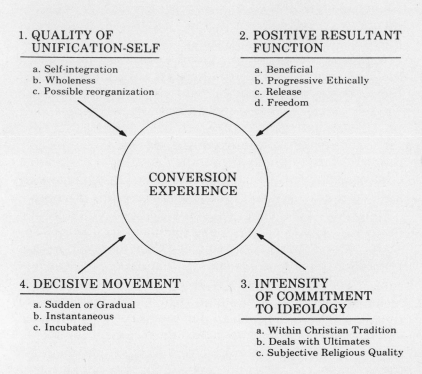

1. QUALITY OF
   UNIFICATION-SELF

   a. Self-integration
   b. Wholeness
   c. Possible reorganization

2. POSITIVE RESULTANT
   FUNCTION

   a. Beneficial
   b. Progressive Ethically
   c. Release
   d. Freedom

CONVERSION
EXPERIENCE

4. DECISIVE MOVEMENT

   a. Sudden or Gradual
   b. Instantaneous
   c. Incubated

3. INTENSITY
   OF COMMITMENT
   TO IDEOLOGY

   a. Within Christian Tradition
   b. Deals with Ultimates
   c. Subjective Religious Quality

probably not be too comprehensive. But looking at the constituent elements in the process provides an observable base for understanding and allows one to examine the various causes and contexts wherein religious conversion is manifest. Therefore, conversion is evident when the above-listed elements are in operation. This does not take into account those whose religious conversions are pathological in nature, wherein the experience may not culminate in positive results; these changes can be examined according to their causes and explained by them. Nevertheless, if at least most of the elements listed are present, it is safe to define the experience as religious conversion. God is active in this change, in this return, but it is not explained totally by "a feeling" about God. Now a closer look at the elements themselves.

UNIFYING QUALITY

This element in religious conversion stresses the *function* of the process itself, taking into consideration earlier definitions that reflect this aspect of conversion. Religious conversion is seem as providing for the emerging self, integrity, and the experience of completeness. This process of becoming whole internally then includes all aspects of "unselfing," disintegration, reflection, reorientation, and recommitment. Jones suggests that the process of conversion would perhaps better be described as a reintegration, a return to one's self, for in this psychological sense, reintegration implies a return to a former state of completeness. This position is a difficult one to maintain psychologically. She suggests however that "in a religious sense, 'return' is a helpful concept if we are clear as to precisely what is meant. That in a wider sense all religious conversion is a return to, a reorganization and appropriation of the source of that which is."[6] In a more restricted sense, some have suggested that conversion is a return to the original teachings from childhood later rejected in adolescence."[7] This concept of conversion as a return would not fit many of the conversion examples throughout history or recorded in the Bible. Although Pascal and Augustine might fit this definition, Paul certainly would not. Yet, the concept of return is biblical, and reflects this theological understanding of the Old Testament view of man alluded to earlier. Since we are to be with God, since reconciliation through Jesus Christ in the N.T. sense reflects this reunion with God, it is a good concept to use in understanding this change. One does in a sense return to God, back to the place from which he came, back to the home of God.

When one is confronted by what someone considers to be infinite and makes a positive move in lining his life up with that perception of a way of life, something integrating happens to him. This change, intense, deep, and profound, this reorganization and reorientation involves the whole of man and is important, while it may or may not be permanent. James in his *Religious Experience* suggests that permanence not be the requirement of effectiveness of experience.

One word, before I close this lecture, on the question of the transiency or permanence of these abrupt conversions. Some of you, I feel sure, knowing that the numerous backslidings and relapses take place, make of these their apperceiving mass for interpreting the whole subject, and dismiss it with a pitying smile as so much "hysterics." Psychologically, as well as religiously, however, this is shallow. It misses the point of serious interest, which is not so much the duration as the nature and quality of these shiftings of character to higher levels. Men lapse from every level—we need no statistics to tell us that. Love is, for instance, well known not to be irrevocable, yet, constant or inconstant, it reveals new flights and reaches of ideality while it lasts.... So with the conversion experience; that it should for even a short time show a human being what the high-water mark of his spiritual capacity is, this is what the high-water mark of his spiritual capacity is, this is what constitutes its importance—an importance which backsliding cannot diminish, although persistence might increase it.[8]

It is interesting to note that James himself in his study found *no* instances of backsliding among those he studied. He gives an example of a M. Ratisbonne, whose whole future was shaped by the few minutes of conversion decision; he subsequently gave up his project of marriage, became a priest, went to Jerusalem, and found a mission field to work for the Jews. The experience was finding of identity—for him, a wholistic, integrating, new selfhood through the process of religious conversion. And Starbuck suggests that the effect of conversion is to "bring with it a changed attitude towards life, which is fairly constant and permanent, although the feelings fluctuate."[9]

RESULTS AND THE LIFE

Any deep change, brought on by any of hundreds of causes, results in various effects. In religious conversion, the effects are always for the better if only so defined by the one experiencing it. Some psychologists however would be quick to point out that some converts have a reactive, regressive and degenerative experience because of religious change.[10] These may be the overall effects as observed by those analyzing the experience, or when viewing a pathological experience, but for the one experiencing conversion, the results seem to appear positive. The post-crisis process is notable for the clarity of feeling and attentiveness to purpose that accompanies it. For example, those who have experienced religious conversion note the characteristics of the new life: the newness, the revival of cheer and fullness, the developments of positive virtues such as courage and hope. These postcrisis feelings do, however, relate to the temperament of the individual, yet generally do typify conversion experience.[11] Others suggest that the post state can be seen only by its positive results. While Pratt speaks of it as the loss of evil habits, Roberts describes the experience as trust in God and inward harmony. While Weininger delineates a period free of anxiety with a new, clearer perception that includes concerns of brotherly love, James suggests that the results of the converted life are total, final, complete, and in some way irreversible.[12] These reflect the biblical concept that "it is a fearful thing to fall into the hands of the living God,"[13] for those who experienced the divine presence historically have been changed dramatically.

Of the group that Salzman studied, those with neurotic tendencies, the results of religious conversion do not come away sounding as positive for the observer. He suggests that in his group the convert has

(1) . . . an exaggerated, irrational intensity of belief in the new doctrine. (2) The convert is more concerned with the form and doctrine than with the greater principle of his new belief; (3) his attitude toward his previous belief is one of contempt, hatred, and denial, and he rejects the possibility that there might be any truth to it; (4) he is intolerant toward all deviates, with frequent acting-out by denouncing and endangering previous friends and associates; (5) he shows a crusading zeal and a need to involve others by seeking new conversions; and, (6) he engages in masochistic and sadistic activities, displaying a need for martyrdom and self-punishment.[14]

Nevertheless, for the participant in religious conversion even these observed negative results, because of the emotional involvement and intense conviction, are viewed and assumed positive. The inevitable difference may arise from the viewpoint of the observer. Thouless describes just such a concept by saying, "The convert may be impressed by her new feeling of love for everybody; her neighbors may observe only the behavior reaction of walking on the curbstone to avoid contact with ungodly people."[15] George Albert Coe, on the other hand, emphasized the experience and is quoted by James as saying, "What is attained is often an altogether new level of spiritual vitality, a relatively heroic level, in which impossible things have become possible, and new energies and endurances are shown."[16] Thus positive results is a constituent element for conversion. These may be simply new directions and therefore interpreted as "good" by the believer, or because of intensity of commitment and definiteness of experience, decisions to eliminate past problems are incorporated into the individual, and he perceives himself as better. Or he may actually be ethically a better person according to the mores of the society in which he exists, due to the new organization of values.

COMMITMENT AND GROWTH

Not only new ideologies result through religious conversion, but in this element of conversion the intensity of commitment to them is emphasized. This intense commitment is usually thought of as reflecting in some way the Christian tradition, but may as well incorporate subjective qualities of religion as well. This would allow an individual who perceives that the experience of change he has gone through has religious qualities or essence to define it as religious conversion. There is in conversion experience a

perceived "confrontation" and a resultant intense commitment to an ethical, creedal, or ideological framework.
Growth is usually the result. In this confrontation of this
crisis, as Lewis Sherrill points out, "God confronts man."[17]
And in the decision to advance into growth or shrink back
from its perils, possible religious conversion takes place.
Conversion thus would include a loyalty to the new way of
life, to the ideological framework of a group, church, or
organization. But it must include a religious quality. This
may only be perceived by the one converted, or it may be
obviously perceived by those who observe, but it must be
present to be religious conversion. The intensity of belief is
an important factor in conversion as well. Intensity may
take the form of emotionalism, deep concern, insight, or
calm understanding, each with intensity and definiteness.

DECISIVE MOVEMENT

True religious conversion demands movement, whether
a movement toward a total life reorganization or a return
to a former belief and life style. The decision is crucial; it
points to a way to walk that is different and since it also
includes a call toward integration, the decisive element is
suggested. This change can, I believe, be expressed as
either gradual or sudden. Since most discussions about
religious conversion simply stress the suddenness of the
experience and therefore spend the majority of time
analyzing this suddenness, conversion is usually thought of
as this fast, sudden crisis. I must, however, include change
that is *either* gradual or sudden as an element in religious
conversion. If this deep change that causes reorganization
of the self is *always* and *only* sudden, and by sudden is
meant a spur of the moment thing, a wrong impression
has been given. Those who differentiate between sudden

and gradual conversions, each being called religious conversion, do perhaps the best job at defining. It seems a
shame that even James in his great work identified gradual
conversion as a type, then illustrated only sudden varieties.
It is important to note, as does Furgeson, "James was indeed correct in affirming that there are two ways in which
mental results may be accomplished, the way of gradual
growth and the way of more sudden conversion, but he
was probably not correct in affirming that these are
psychologically the same process."[18] The typologies of
sudden and gradual are in themselves misleading for they
do not take into account the possible period of incubation
which leads up to the crisis of change. With this concept,
even sudden experiences of conversion have their gradual
elements. Yet if one studies just the actual change that
comes after conversion experience, that sudden turn-
around in behavior or belief, then the temptation is to list
the experience as sudden, even though the causes may
have been extended far into the prehistory of the event
itself. One perhaps would be true to the term of religious
conversion itself if the exact change and the integration
that takes place directly after the crises were the only
criteria for defining it, but change cannot be totally understood unless the preceding conflicts, wishes, desires, or
circumstances are truly taken into consideration. Or as
Salzman suggests, "most change—possibly all—is gradual
in its development, but since it culminates in a specific
moment of alteration or conversion, it may seem to . . . be
an instantaneous, unexplained, mysterious event. However in every case there has been an incubation or preparation."[19] And the insight of Tillich is as well significant to
this idea.

The image of turning around in one's way produces the
impression of something momentary and sudden, and, in

spite of all pietistic misuse of it, the element of suddenness should not be excluded from a prescription of conversion. It is a decision, and the very word decision points to the momentary act of cutting off other possibilities.[20]

It is evident that the debate as to whether sudden or gradual is the proper adverb to describe the action of conversion will remain one of the larger questions of this book. Few have been willing to let go of the gradual Bushnellian connotations of change of this type, yet it is important to stress that within religious conversion experience, there is a decisive, or crucial moment of change, and this seems to be closer to a proper understanding of the word. This decisive moment in the change is crucial for conversion to be truly in operation within experience. However, if we are to be saved from definitional bedlam we must reassert that the experience of religious conversion has a decisiveness about it often interpreted as sudden and is not the same as gradual growth, yet has many of its aspects, even if only the moment of decision is what is sudden.

The event itself is decisive for it is a personal event, at the core of man's being in that it changes him so drastically. Many may be confronted with ultimate decisions many times, yet perhaps may not acknowledge it or be affected by it. But religious conversion experience asserts a decisiveness about the encounter. Jones suggests that conversion therefore must be the first encounter with "sacred" that man responds to, accepts, digests, absorbs, and actualizes.[21] It is not however the first interest or the normal meeting, but rightly suggests that the meeting is significant in that it is within this experience that man appropriates the power of ultimate Being. This meeting then is the first real mature realization of the fact that things of ultimate value affect the life of man. This decisiveness or cruciality of decision is significant. Now the meanings of life are appropriated to the mind and take on major importance to the convert; the decision to change forms the fabric of life in which all of life is now viewed.

A shift now in our study occurs from the actual understanding of the experience, to the dynamics of the event itself. It is important to note here that in order for a relationship to be properly drawn, significant dynamics, causes, results, must be examined. The following chapter is an attempt to arrive at the actualities that are the underlining dynamics, and centering in on the identity aspects of religious conversion experience before actual discussion of identity formation takes place.

NOTES

1. Sante de Sanctis, *Religious Conversion: A Bio-Psychological Study* (London: Kegan Paul, Trench Trubner & Co., 1927), pp. 92, 115, 127, 142.

2. William Paterson, *Conversion* (New York: Charles Scribner's Sons, 1940), pp. 155–156.

3. George Jackson, *The Fact of Conversion: The Cole Lectures for 1908* (New York: Fleming H. Revell Co., 1908), p. 97.

4. Earl Furgeson, "The Definition of Religious Conversion," *Pastoral Psychology,* XVI (September, 1965), p. 9.

5. See Barbara Eleanor Jones, "Conversion: An Examination of the Myth of Human Change" (unpublished Ph.D. dissertation, Columbia University, 1969), for a detailed accounting of how the terms for religious change have been altered.

6. Barbara Eleanor Jones, "The Myth of Human Change," p. 76.

7. William James, *The Varieties of Religious Experience,* Mentor Books (New York: New American Library of World Literature, Inc., 1958), p. 205.

8. Ibid.

9. E. D. Starbuck, *The Psychology of Religion* (New York: Charles Scribner's Sons, 1915), pp. 357–360. In addition to this, Starbuck found that as he collected facts on the duration of conversion experienced from some one hundred subjects, more than half Methodists, 93 percent of the women and 77 percent of the men had been backsliders before their conversion. Starbuck concluded that people experiencing conversion once having taken their stand and identified with a church do not leave it even if their previous enthusiasm declines.

10. Furgeson, "Religious Conversion," p. 8.

11. George Barton Cutten, *The Psychological Phenomena of Christianity* (New York: Charles Scribner's Sons, 1908), p. 250.

12. Starbuck, *The Psychology of Religion,* pp. 123–124; James Bisset Pratt, *The Religious Consciousness: A Psychological Study* (New York: Macmillan Co., 1926), pp. 162–163; David E. Roberts, *Psychotherapy and a Christian View of Man* (New York: Charles Scribner's Sons, 1950); Benjamin Weininger, "The Interpersonal Factor in the Religious Experience," *Psychoanalysis* (March, 1955), p. 31; James, *Religious Experience,* pp. 195–207.

13. Hebrews 10:31.

14. Leon Salzman, "Types of Religious Conversion," *Pastoral Psychology,* XVII (1966), p. 18.

15. Robert H. Thouless, *An Introduction to the Psychology of Religion* (Cambridge: Cambridge University Press, 1971), p. 113.

16. James, *Religious Experience,* p. 194.

17. Lewis Joseph Sherrill, *The Struggle of the Soul* (New York: Macmillan Co., 1951), p. 27.

18. Furgeson, "Religious Conversion," p. 10.

19. Leon Salzman, "The Psychology of Regressive Religious Conversions," *Journal of Pastoral Care,* VIII, No. 2 (1954), p. 63.

20. Paul Tillich, *Systematic Theology* (3 Vols: Chicago: University of Chicago Press, 1951–63), III, p. 220.

21. Jones, "Human Change," p. 69.

CHAPTER III

LIFE: The Context of Change

"Religion is not so much theology as life. It is to be lived rather than reasoned about." James Pratt.

"A Presbyterian middle-class teenager raised in a conservative church in a southern city will probably be more like a Scots middle-class teenager raised in a conservative church in Scotland than the American Presbyterian teenager will be like a liberal Jewish teenager raised in the same southern town. In this case, the southern town presents us with the same society for the Jewish and the Presbyterian teenager. However, the primary society (conservative Presbyterian church) interprets a religious tradition (Calvinism) in such a way that another teenager raised in a similar religious environment, though it be four thousand miles away, will be more like the American Presbyterian than the latter will be like his liberal Jewish fellow citizen." C. Ellis Nelson.

Since the form of religious conversion experience most easily observed is the sudden variety—like the kind with rather abrupt and immediate behavioral change—little is said about the dynamics operant in conversion of the more gradual variety, the reason being the unavailability of observation over long periods of time. Life changes people slowly at times as Pratt suggests, but still the intensity of change seems deep, the commitment to ideology equally intense, yet because of its nature, little is said as to the dynamics that are functioning in this situation. Sudden experience, however, has been more thoroughly studied, as will be reflected in this chapter.

Major contributions to the knowledge of religious conversion appeared early in the century beginning with Hall, James, and Starbuck. With the beginning of the study of behaviorism, little of scientific value was accomplished until the resurgence of psychodynamic methods and insight. Writers concerned with the psychology of religious conversion see that the experience does not just happen; it is caused. Man usually is not struck outside his situation, and therefore, it would seem that understanding the suggested psychological dynamics involved with religious conversion would aid immensely in understanding the relationship with identity.

Most writers see several factors operant in religious conversion experience—the individual's environment, past and present situations, the very psyche of the person, pathology, as well as the divine.[1] Others, such as James or Salzman, deal with the issue of distinguishing the validity of the experience according to its results.[2] Hiltner suggests that the turning around may be a political or economic, as well as a religious, kind of event and still be a conversion experience. And according to our definition, if subjectively perceived as "religious," the event could be classified as religious conversion if all the dynamics are present. No real turning point is without antecedents, such as dissatisfaction with the status quo or lure from an ideal. With the modern insights of psychodynamics and social psychology, the actual internal process may very well be traced. The religious conversion may be seen as conflict-resolution, in one sphere or many, and thus stem from an emotional context, while other more secular forms of change or conversions may have their roots in observable social forms. In looking at religious conversion, others may see an effective cause in developmental sources, and yet another group see psychological factors and theories operant in the change. One may be converted to communism, the John Birch Society, the Alcoholics Anonymous, jazz, Mahler, or many other things other than the Christian faith. This should not be confused with religious conversion and could better be called just change perhaps, but the intensity demands its use. For in no instance does the actual event of turning around itself attest to the soundness of the new ideology which is espoused. For a decision of that kind, other criteria than personal experience are needed. Likewise, the occurrence of the experience in no way validates religious conversion itself. Others interested in validation and truth must decide this. The authority on which "truth" is validated is personal and even for some, revealed. Understanding how one makes something or someone an authority cannot be discussed here, although it would provide an interesting research topic for another book. But first a discussion of the experience itself.

EXPERIENTIAL KNOWING

There are many accounts of religious conversion experience, most recorded in the history of religion. Apostle Paul is cited as a chief example; Augustine of Hippo and Pascal are others. Little current research has recorded the experiential factors of the happening. Dr. John Lilly does an excellent job of describing drug-induced experiences in his volume, *The Center of the Cyclone: An Autobiography of Inner Space,* but the changes induced here in personality were from external sources, drugs, and later, meditation.[3] These experiences, although related to experiences labeled conversion, do not fit the definition entirely, due to their chemical relationship to the biochemistry of the individual partaking of them.

The religious conversion experience itself may be divided into three phases: (1) preconversion experience, (2) crisis, and (3) postconversion. Each has distinctive parts. First, in the preconversion stage, such feelings as intense intrapsychic conflict (causes of this state will be discussed under social context), a distinctive sense of unrest, dissatisfaction with self, a vague lack in the life of some kind, a general feeling of discontent or a feeling of wanting something or wanting to be something that is not yet clear to oneself, is evident.[4] Starbuck recognized that the preconvert suffered from a sense of dividedness ". . . the contrast between what is, and what might be. . . ."[5] Leuba and Starbuck during the same time in history describe the religious conversion experience in great detail showing the initial period as one of anxiety, doubt, depression, or guilt. There is as well a state of tension that exists, perhaps brought on by the dissonance between certain feelings that he is unable to reconcile with his traditional, culturally-determined world view. There is an acute intensification of the discomfort that occurs, then frequently a feeling of the "awesome," the "uncanny," which is interpreted as a religious communication.[6]

Thouless, regarding Paul's experience, suggests that it is worthy to note in his preconversion experience there was an intensified hostility exhibited, shown in his persecution of Christians.[7] In Starbuck's early studies of 1899, he found the most prominent experiences in the preconversion state to be in descending order depression, pensive sadness, calling on God, restless anxiety and uncertainty, sense of sin, loss of sleep or appetite, feelings of estrangement from God, desire for a better life, doubt and question, earnest seriousness, weeping, and nervousness.[8] Sense of sin seemed to be predominant in adolescent religious conversion experiences as well, and this sin was very vivid. The conflict that arises from wishing one was something else, and the knowledge of what one really is, is significant here, for part of the emotional experience of conversion is that one's previous life appears so bad. This may even be one reason that conversion stories are told with such vividness in revivals, for their potency for change may very well be reliant upon the more dramatic abandonment of sin, which is more easily eliminated when the audience sees the depth of the sin and the greater distance the listeners are from the goal proposed by the evangelist. Even though this agonizing period precedes the experience and may be evident gradually over long periods of time or come rather suddenly, the period seems necessary for change, if only for reflection. Deep change may not be forthcoming through this one instance of agony, but conflict tends to break old patterns and thus leads the way for deep change. It would seem logical to assert that this may be the reason for the conflict in conversional change. What must, however, be pointed out is that unity exists with much unique variety, as in all realms of living. There are many marked differences in each experience, and the above prestate can only be taken as outlining general areas of early emotional stress which may lead to this returning to God.

There are marked differences in the time taken to effect changes in individuals. For example, impressions differed widely among those experiencing religious conversion regarding the most dominant feelings in the preconversion state, which was also evident in the nature of the blessings converts believed they had received, as well as in the attributing source for the conversion. In reply to the question, "In what did the change consist?" Starbuck's group found "forgiveness" in first place by 16 percent and "oneness with friends," 14 percent.[9] Salzman points out that of those in his regressive category, or those with pathological bases for change in religious conversion, most had feelings of hatred, resentment, and hostility. Destructive attitudes were in each case he examined and he stresses that the role of hatred in conversion is as true for the mentally imbalanced as conflict or lack of identity is for the more normal person.[10] Even through his negative assessment of religious conversion source, he correctly sees the close identity-forming function of the religious change.

Moving from the preconversion state into the crisis phase itself, James recorded the feelings which immediately filled the hour of the religious conversion experience as being primarily a sense of a higher control; he called this the "subliminal other."[11] This concept was validated by the more recent studies of Carl Christensen, who suggests that Edoardo Weiss's concept of the "psychic" presence is applicable here and forms a useful hypothesis explaining this subjective feeling. (Briefly, the psychic presence is thought to be the nonegotized mental image of another person which affects the individual's emotions and behavior.) The religious convert would never accept such a statement. The presence is supernatural to be sure for the convert. This presence was not always there, however, in Christiansen's studies: "A part of the conversion experience included a sense of presence. The intensity of this subjective feeling varied from person to person, some vague, others a definite sense of someone being close by . . . it is a part of the convert's concept of God."[12]

Sometimes among various Pentacostal groups the believer senses something that is different and extraordinary. For this group, glossolalia has sometimes been present

along with religious conversion and becomes the validi-
fying mark of the experience. The believer feels that there
must be God present because of the miracle of linguistics.[13]
Starbuck found the central factors in the experience itself
to be spontaneous awakening, forgiveness, public confession, a sense of oneness and sameness, determination and
direction, and self-surrender.[14] This last factor of self-
surrender is a important experiential factor in the experience. This "giving up" and final choice is the event
that resolves the crisis. The decision to change is significant, then, to the release of the crisis and to complete
conversion. James quotes Starbuck and suggests the following dialogue by a convert regarding this self-surrender.

> "I had said I would not give up; but when my will was
> broken, it was all over".... Another says: "I simply said:
> 'Lord, I have done all I can; I leave the whole matter with
> thee'; and immediately there came to me a great peace."—
> Another: "All at once it occurred to me that I might be saved,
> too, if I would stop trying to do it all myself, and follow Jesus:
> somehow I lost my load."—Another: (")I finally ceased to re-
> sist, and gave myself up, though it was a hard struggle.
> Gradually the feeling came over me that I had done my part,
> and God was willing to do his."—"Lord, Thy will be done;
> damn or save!" cries John Nelson, exhausted with the anxious
> struggle to escape damnation; and at that moment his soul
> was filled with peace.[15]

The sense of giving up has been equated with the form
of submitting to authority, interpreted as God. Christensen even suggests it is a form of giving up to the mother
image.[16] The self-surrender is brought on by the feeling of
conviction of sin. Up to this point the person may be aware
of his feelings exhibited in the preconversion state, those
of incompleteness, doubt, alienation, restlessness, and anxiety. When realizing that he is convicted of sin, or simply

responsible himself for himself and in his helplessness, stands alone before divine presence, his being suffers and this suffering is conviction of sin; the release is brought about by self-surrender. Starbuck's reasons for self-surrender seem appropriate.

> To begin with, there are two things in the mind of the candidate for conversion: The present incompleteness or wrongness, the "sin" which he is eager to escape from; and second, the positive ideal which he longs to compass. Now with most of us the sense of present wrongness is a far more distinct piece of our consciousness than is the imagination of any positive ideal we can aim at. In a majority of cases, indeed, the "sin" almost exclusively engrosses the attention, so that conversion is a process of struggling away from sin rather than a striving towards righteousness.[17]

There are other experiences accompanying religious conversion. Such things as hallucinations, visions, photisms even are seen, but always conviction, self-surrender and crisis seem to be commonalities with the experience itself. After the crisis comes a moment of turning. And it is here that the experience and the word itself come together. Crisis here is essential to the turning for man. It seems that times of accounting are inherent within the structure of living, and growth seems to be associated with turning points.[18] And since life is growth itself, crises are inevitable. The points of turning may not be acute or especially dramatic, but they are real and are seen as events. "The crisis is understood to be capitulated by similar factors as the preconversion period; ... the crisis is seen as the source from which the rest flows, rather than merely the point from which the results are marked."[19] The resolution of the crisis, or the solution of the struggle between the higher and lower parts of man's nature, using theological language, is the endeavor on the part of the convert to make the new ideology, or concepts, or way of life his very own. This may be contrary to his habit patterns and life style and this precipitates the struggle and crisis. Cutten suggests that in some, rather than a sense of sin before surrender, the term of conviction should be used to describe this feeling attitude. This may last for weeks or for hours or days and may appear with varying degrees of intensity, yet is always determined and definite.[20] For Starbuck, the conversion phenomena of conviction of sin last about one-fifth as long as the periods of adolescent storm and stress phenomena, for which he had statistics. This stress period in religious conversion is not as long, yet much more intense. Bodily accompaniments enjoined the experience, such as loss of sleep and appetite. These signs of stress and unrest were more prominent in adolescence.[21]

The act of giving in, decision, resolution, of crisis sublimination, or any other term, results in the final state of conversion, the postexperience briefly stated in Chapter II. James calls the result resolution of stress a "state of assurance rather than a 'faith-state.' Central to the experience was the loss of all worry, a sense of ultimate well-being, peace, harmony, the willingness to be, even though outer conditions should remain the same. A new certainty of God's grace ensued and a passion of willingness of acquiescence, of admiration followed."[22] A typical description of this experience is recorded by Tillich.

This process of conversion has not turned my world upside down, although at times it has seemed to do so. It has, instead, set me on my feet again, whereas for nearly half a century I was trying to think things out while standing on my head; there is this pervasive quality to the appropriative encounter: all of man is transformed in a total reconstruction.[23]

This experience is called a "postdisaster Utopia" or post-crisis feeling, and is noted for its clarity, liberating sense and healing potential.[24] Starbuck cites such feeling as joy, peace, acceptance and oneness with God or Christ, a new happiness, bodily lightness, weeping or shouting, partial relief, a sense of responsibility or a sense of redirection and subdued calm. Of the 151 men studied, 43 mentioned a result as being a closer relation to God, 4 suggested a closer feeling of knowing Christ, 34 suggested a closer relation with nature, and 42 found a closer love for others or a desire to help others. Of women surveyed the results were substantially the same.[25]

When one undergoes a serious crisis and its subsequent resolution, a natural sense of relief is found and with it comes the desire to share it with others. This too is an aspect of religious conversion experience. An experience of this nature is not valid until it is shared, for one function of commitment is witness to that conviction.

The postcrisis feelings are related to the surrender act as its cause. In answer to why the positive phase follows religious conversion, Tiebout suggests this answer based on his dealings with alcoholics:

> I know the positive phase comes, but not just why. Surrender means cessation of fight and cessation of fight seems logically to be followed by internal peace and quiet. That point seems fairly obvious, but why the whole feeling tone switches from negative to positive with all the concomitant changes is not so clear. Nevertheless, despite my inability to explain the phenomenon, there is no question that the change does take place and that it may be initiated by an act of surrender.[26]

The surrender then, triggers reactions with the person and his perception of life changes. For him the world is different; its difference may simply be the new look of things through eyes of faith, but the newness brings meaning that the observer never before experienced. James refers to a "shifting of man's centers of personal energy" in this same vein.[27] But under any terminology, the result is problem-solving and identity-forming. It seems tragic that the realm of religious experience for many psychologists has fallen into the area of the abnormal and psychologically unhealthy. The evidence of religion is not in fact real evidence of any pathology. For the religious conversion experience in its problem-solving function and identity-forming aspect serves as a framework for maturity in coping with the problems of living and eternity. Religious beliefs fulfill many of the basic needs of mankind in that they motivate human behavior. Because of this they are therefore subject to investigation and psychiatric scrutiny. Again Christensen's claim comes to mind: "Since psychiatry is concerned with mental disorders, much of the psychiatric contributions to the understanding of religious beliefs have emphasized psychopathology. Sometimes, psychiatrists tend to forget that religion is a normal part of man's individual and cultural life."[28]

Another factor in looking at the experience is the notion that the convert feels religious conversion to be something that was not brought on by will or reason. In Starbuck's study, 23 percent felt that the awakening into new life was a spontaneous happening like a bursting forth without any apparent cause. While only a surprising 10 percent gave credit to God, 11 percent recalled the experience as a self-surrender in which they themselves actually participated.[29] Those who found a more gradual conversional change to their personality construct saw the volitional powers dominate the judgment in the change.[30] James gave credit to unconscious factors, in the psychoanalytic tradition, as prefactors for religious conversion.[31] It is evident, in many cases, that change is brought about through factors unseen to the rational mind. Those with newer existential viewpoints such as Allport, Maslow, and Carl Rogers however stress the role of conscious, present decision for behavior change, but as important as this willing-of-behavior is, early life situations, genetics, intelligence, culture, and environment are factors in any kind of change that cannot be negated and therefore play a role in the effective results.

In summary then, the experience of religious conversion is outlined in these stages: the *initial* or *preconversion*, signified by the tension and questioning of role and being, including emotions of anxiety and stress; the *crisis*, thought of in terms of conviction of sin, or confrontation with answers to ponderous questions; and the *postconversion* stage where answers are found, relief is felt, release of problems is experienced, and confusion is lifted. The convert feels himself renewed, redirected, integrated, and fully functioning. This rather sudden climax typifies the religious conversion experience; however, in the more gradual form of conversion (the slow building up of tension, or the gradual growing into faith), many of the same elements of the sudden variety are shown. The usual feelings regarding conviction, surrender, and assurance are operant even though they grow to a peak at the decision moment. The decision may not be momentous, but the effect is equally as releasing. And as James suggests, the most characteristic of all of the elements for the religious conversion crisis and the "last of which I speak, is the ecstasy of happiness produced."[32] The results seem the same.

EMOTIONAL FEELINGS

The role of the emotions in causing behavioral change has long been studied. Since religious conversion deals with the core of man and changes man so drastically, emotions, too, are factors in experiencing conversion. W. H. Clark, after stating that Freud remarks that beliefs acquired through emotional experiences are removed only by an equally intense outpouring of emotion, proposes the concept of "conversion shock" as the emotional dynamic in the abrupt change.[33] And Mogar believes that the bulk of the research indicates that the intensity of the experience rather than the contents determines change.[34] Even early studies such as James's *Religious Experience* hinted at the dynamics of emotion involved in the change experience. William James, quoting one of Starbuck's correspondents, writes, for instance:

> I have been through the experience which is known as conversion. My explanation of it is this: the subject works his emotions up to the breaking point, at the same time resisting their physical manifestations, such as quickened pulse, etc., and then suddenly lets them have their full sway over his body. The relief is something wonderful, and the pleasurable effects of the emotions are experienced to the highest degree.[35]

It is important to stress here that the religious excitement brought about by such situations is not conversion; only when it results in a new look at life, as a reintegration of being, a change, does it fulfill the term. Religious conversion is more than the product of nervous instability or the expression of moral need. It is deep form of change.[36]
The relationship of emotions to the dynamics of reli-

gious conversion has received extensive study. The dynamics of emotion are assumed to be operant factors in the experience itself, if not a chief cause. For example, there is some evidence that suggestibility follows and is enhanced through the pressures of emotions such as stress. Intense emotion lessens inhibitions and contributes to suggestibility. This is Sargent's major theme, for he sees religious conversion the result of a mental abreaction in which the mind is simply overloaded with emotion. And it seems there is evidence that the involvement and excitement that accompanies involvement increases a person's susceptibility to change, especially if the situation requires that participant to assume some initiative.[37] The relationship of suggestion and persuasion will be discussed in more detail in the section analyzing environmental and revivalistic factors.

Religious conversion is by some diagrammed in a conflict-resolution model. There are conflicts building up in the preconversion state that strive toward resolution. Since conversion is usually seen in a religious context of some kind or another, the conflict oftentimes centers around values and takes the form of a choice between them. There are mental processes which actively resist change—changes of belief, ideology, behavior, cause, or intention. Thouless suggests that it is this conflict that man tends to rationalize. The convert-to-be may rationalize the systems offered to him, as contrary evidence is presented, as the basis for a new attitude. The conflict may be strong when the holder may be unwilling to give up the comforts of certain convictions and to pass through the "unpleasant and insecure condition of doubt. He may also be unwilling to give up the comfort and security he received from his membership of the social group to which he belonged."[38]

Salzman considered these conversions brought on through pressures related to conflict to be in his regressive type of conversion experience, for it is an attempt to solve the pressing and serious problems in living, or a way of dealing with extreme disintegrating conflict. Regardless of the conflictive base for the change, it is a pseudo-solution, and he speculates that it is likely to occur in neurotic, pre-psychotic, or psychotic persons. He, however, is not consistent in suggesting this personality correlate for religious conversion when he adds that it may also occur in presumably normal people when they are faced with major conflicts or insuperable difficulties.[39] The process at work in this conflict-model may actually result in normality and a better coping with life and therefore be a positive influence for the individual as Boisen suggests. Salzman is perhaps correct in assuming that if the results are caused from pathology or psychopathology and result in regressive tendencies, they are not normal. Perhaps only a trained analyst can distinguish between the progressive form and regressive form; I certainly would not want to generalize here.

Conflict stems from many sources: doubt—when the person feels that his life seems more of an expression of human interest than divine; stress—when a person feels inadequate and is unsettled within his mind; tension—produced from a number of sources (family, the church, one's conscious or unconscious lack). Sargent points out that those who want to eliminate erroneous beliefs and undesirable behavior patterns, then implant saner beliefs and attitudes, are more likely to achieve success if they can first induce nervous tension or stir up sufficient feelings of anger or anxiety in order to secure the person's undivided attention. This action increases his suggestibility. He feels that by increasing or prolonging stress, inducing physical debilitation, a more thorough alteration of the person's thinking processes will be achieved.

The immediate effect of such treatment is, usually, to impair judgment and increase suggestibility . . . . When the tension is removed the suggestibility likewise diminishes, yet ideas implanted while it lasted may remain. If the stress or the psychical debilitation, or both, are carried one stage further, it may happen that patterns of thought and behavior, especially those of recent acquisition, become disrupted. New patterns can then be substituted or suppressed patterns allowed to reassert themselves; or the subject may begin to act or think in ways that precisely contradict his former ones.[40]

This would validate the use of psychological weapons in the attempts by some groups to get change through the use of such things as fasting, chastening of the flesh by scourging, drumming, dancing, singing, music, inducement of fear, lighting incense, drugs. There seem to be many ways to alter normal brain functions for religious purposes as James's nitrous oxide interest testifies. Sargent charges that few sects wholly neglect the role of these emotional psychological stimulants for change.[41]

The role of conflict in religion has biblical imagery. The story of Jacob and the night wrestling match and encounter with God is an example. But this conflict of wishing you were one thing and knowing you are another is severe and produces tension that may find release in the religious conversion experience.

Other forms of conflict and tension are exhaustion caused by the struggle and thus weakening the power of the mind to integrate happenings consistently, and fear brought on from external circumstances as well. It is commonly realized that the great evangelists of the previous eras, such as Jonathan Edwards and John Wesley, dwelt on the horrors of damnation, while some modern evangelistic movements use more subtle means of producing fear. Many a student of homiletics is acquainted with Jonathan Edwards's famous sermon, "Sinners in the Hand of an Angry God." His preaching has been most unjustly judged by it. Many have read with fear and anxiety the following phrases:

> And though he will know that you cannot bear the weight of omnipotence treading upon you, yet he will not regard that, but he will crush out your blood, and make it fly, and it shall be sprinkled on his garments, so as to stain all his raiment. He will not only hate you but will have you in the utmost contempt; no place shall be fit for you, but under his feet to be trodden down as the mire of the streets.[42]

It is no wonder that Edwards has been accused of confusing God with the devil! Fear arousal of this kind causes great conflict within. Man's natural reaction is release in situations like these, a release that religious conversion can perhaps provide. Ducasse suggested that in the intrapsychic conflict, a need for commitment, guilt, and fear were necessary factors for a religious conversion. In addition, he felt that there was a sense of failure involved with the fear, based on the inability to conform to the demands religion made. This inability to conform produced depression, therefore contributing to the tension and anxiety.[43] Salzman adds a twist to this, indicating that fear is the dynamic involved and suggests that hate could be the motivational factor to consider.[44] Salzman suggests that this hate motivation has been repeated on a smaller scale throughout the history of the development of religious doctrines. The mass hysteria caused by thoughts of werewolves and witches not only caused the deaths of werewolves and witches, but produced a large number of so-called conversions in the prevailing churches and *into* the ranks of witches as well. The contagious and widespread nature of the conversions during such community hate programs indicated the extent of the hatred, and may very well be a strong cause along with suggestion in many conversions.[45]

It is also believed that, especially in the frontier revivals, an emotional stimulus evident in conversions was that of "escape." The success of the evangelistic meetings in early American settlements was that they offered the readiest means for the hard-working pioneer to find an escape from his everyday drudgery into a world of temporary exhilaration; this of course is only speculation, but could be factual if operant in the experience was an active *seeking* for release from the everyday work of the frontier. For like satisfaction of other desires, conversion may fulfill the need for new experience with peculiar intensity and fullness in these kinds of situations.[46]

It would seem then that the presence of an emotional matrix can be significant for religious conversion experience. Forces in conflict, stress, tension, fear, anxiety, feelings of intense inadequacy often precede the conversion crisis. The conflict seems to be a conscious one, even though its sources may find roots in the unconscious conflict which simply adds to the intrapsychic stress. In addition to this, there seems to be additional contexts wherein religious conversion occurs. Among these is the developmental context.

DEVELOPMENTAL BECOMING

Adolescence

It has often been suggested that adolescence is the most favorable time for religious conversion.[47] The uniqueness of the age itself, the time in the development of the self, and the conflict orientation of that period of time have been observed. Regarding religious maturity of this age, much has been said. The Catholic satirist Alexander Pope in part suggested

> Behold the child, by nature's kindly law,
> Pleased with a rattle, tickled with a straw;
> Some livelier plaything gives his youth delight,
> A little louder, but as empty quite:
> Scarfs, garters, gold, amuse his riper stage,
> And beads and prayer-books are the toys of age.
> ("An Essay on Man," Epistle II, 11. 275–280.)

It is in the lives of youth where one finds the wonder and spontaneous religious commitment. These characteristics have described the great religions of man and are essential parts of the religious conversion experience.

It was Starbuck who first drew attention through studies that the incidence of religious conversion was the highest in the age of adolescence. Observing this, he felt that normal religious conversions were therefore adolescent phenomena and recognized that fear, guilt, and depression preceded the reaction. Some take a broad approach which loses significance since the whole process of change in adolescence is equated with general conversion. Pratt saw adolescence as a normal period for the experience although he minimizes the violent and sudden adolescent religious conversion experience in suggesting that the entire "moral and religious process of the adolescent period may well be called conversion."[48]

Studies using empirical methods have tended to agree as to adolescence being a prominent age for conversion.

There have been other studies dealing with numbers of converts, but not dealing specifically with the age of con-

CHART 1. List of studies and relative age-time computations.

Name:	Cases:	Average Age:
Starbuck (1899)	1,265	16.4
Coe (1900)	1,784	16.4
Hall (1904)	4,054	16.6
Athearn (1924)	6,194	14.6
Clark, E. T. (1929)	2,174	12.7
Argyle (1959)	Study of Literature	15.0

version. For example, E. T. Clark in 1929 and Gordon Allport in 1948 found that only about 7 percent of the college population had experienced sudden conversion. These authorities find adolescence the natural time for the experience. However, just how one defines conversion may modify this conclusion. For example, if conversion is termed in its gradual form and includes turning points and times of decisions, later times may be indicated. Jung in 1933 found that the middle age and after were the prime years for the religious decision and the largest growth in religious things. His views received some support from Fuerst (1966), who questioned some seventy-five subjects that were over fifty years of age and reported that turning points in general occur at various ages throughout life.[49] Since the studies of Argyle, the American Institute of Public Opinion (AIPO) polled a national sample of Americans on sudden "religious or mystic" experiences, and found about 20 percent of the adults answered affirmatively and could describe such an experience.[50] Using content analysis, five kinds of experience were found: (1) a mystical sense of union with God, (2) a

conviction of forgiveness and salvation, (3) answers to
prayers, (4) reassurances of God's power and (5) dreams
and voices.[51]

Twice-born experiences have seemed to be normative
for youth. Probably the most effective longitudinal study
ever attempted in this area was by Charles Stewart. His
concern of early studies led him to spend 1962–1963 at the
Menninger Foundation in alliance with the Child Study
Project. Here he had the occasion to study youth from a
variety of religious backgrounds and with many different
variables of growth and nurture as they entered puberty.
From this he drew case studies and inferences for a psychology of religious conversion. He points out various developmental factors evident in conversion experience and
contributory to its occurrence. In contrasting boys and
girls, he suggests each undergo puberty with primary sexual maturation. The menstrual cycle in girls begins between ages eleven and one-half to thirteen, and the first
seminal emission occurs in boys between ages twelve and
one-half and fourteen. The secondary sexual characteristics such as physique, timber of voice, and auxiliary hair,
etc., are paralleled in both the boys and girls. The young
adolescent is, in the period immediately following puberty,
undergoing changes from his external struggles to the
inner conflicts that he feels from his burgeoning sexual
drives and the ambivalences he feels regarding his parents.
These affect the religious sensibilities.[52] Arnold Gesell
says:

> As the adolescent enters his teens he often recurs to quiet,
> meditative periods of self-examination. He has earnest
> moments of high resolve and aspiration. He begins to define
> himself by matching it with that of other selves. He explores
> his potentials in terms of self-chosen heroes and ideals.
> Thereby he gives precision and status to his feelings.[53]

One crucial problem of this age is that of identifying what kind of adult he is becoming and what sort of life is to be of the greatest satisfaction to himself, along with various other developmental tasks that affect the adolescent emotional growth. First, the adolescent must learn to accept his own physique and determine the place of new relationships with age-mates of both sexes; these tasks are social in nature. The social tasks to be mastered in this area are often defined by each culture and subculture and many times develop almost naturally within the subculture.

Secondly, the adolescent must develop independence from his parents and other adults. This area of development finds anxiety running high, and the feeling tones and stress existing in this period prove intense. In seeking a certain amount of independence comes the concern of other forms of independence, such as economical, occupational, intellectual. At this time the adolescent finds that he must think of a proper ideology appropriate for later marriage and family life, and values need to be firmly fixed into the mind of the youth. These decisions prove difficult for some youth, and anxiety and conflict emerge as the concomitant emotions.

Havighurst continues his developmental task chronology by listing the following tasks for early adulthood, adding possible additional sources for conflict after adolescence, such as: (1) selecting a mate; (2) learning to live with a marriage partner; (3) starting a family; (4) rearing children; (5) managing a home; (6) getting started in an occupation; (7) taking a civic responsibility; (8) finding a congenial social group.[54]

The developing adolescent finds that along with the physical growth which causes implications within the social sphere, there is growing intelligence, which tends to stimulate and release a new kind of questioning spirit. The Newsom Report states graphically:

> Boys and girls who used to ask enquiringly, "What do we do?" or "What's that" now commonly react with "Why should I?" or "How do you know?" to much of what they have loved and practiced in the past. They become increasingly aware of the differences of opinion between adults and of the gulf between practice and profession. The borderline between cynical disengagement and constructive questioning is narrow.[55]

This kind of questioning about life is further encouraged by the mass media. Television, for example, in the new programming for adolescents, deals with problems thought above and too mature for the adolescent age only a few years ago. The historical context of the times also is reflected in the adolescent behavior. Greater freedom of growth and respect *from* their elders has aided in this. There are basic needs that are suggested in this period which need fulfilling in order for the complete integration with life and reality to take place. The need for security, with its concomitant feelings of freedom, is important. Status as well is evident in the hierarchy of needs for the youth. A youth finds himself in the worst of all possible worlds—being neither an adult nor a child—he seeks to find meaning in life within his social and mental context. The youth also has needs in the area of relationships. Love, for example, is being quested; love that a group, or a tradition, or a belief can provide. Religious conversion may fill this need. The young person searches for meaning in all of the activities and ideologies of life. The years of adolescence, from twelve to sixteen, are a watershed in the emergence of an ideological framework for later life.

In M. H. Podd's study in ego identity, he interviewed
134 male college juniors and seniors. J. E. Marcia followed
with identity interviews covering occupational choice, religious beliefs, and political ideology. "Crisis" and "commitment" were assessed in each of these areas to define
each identity status of the youth. The implications of this
study are essential to the development of the theses in this
book. In essence, the morally-transitional subjects were
changing with regard to identity issues as well as moral
issues. Or stated more clearly, in order to question the
conventional morality you must have questioned your
identity as well. In other words, the adolescent questioning
of moral issues and his concerns as to what is reality is
central to the adolescent's identity concerns. Podd suggests
as a sideline that morally-conventional subjects have a considerable likelihood of never having an identity crisis or an
identity questioning at all.[56] It would appear then in relation to the concerns of this book that the adolescent nature
to question morally-centered things would be directly related to the religious conversion experience, providing
there is a similarity in the kind of crisis faced in adolescence and the nature of religious conversion in this age
group. Religious conversion would then provide the
framework for crisis in adolescence which contributes to
the identity formation of the youth themselves.

Adolescence is a time for adjusting conformities and trying to sort out what is to be instituted into one's ideological
framework and what is to be rejected totally. Various
motivations exist within the adolescent then, physically,
emotionally, intellectually, ideologically, developmentally
motivated actions.

Such pressures for change are illustrated in this discussion of the thinking of one adolescent regarding her conversion experience. Notice especially her ambivalence to

understand her true motives, yet the concomitant decisiveness regarding her mother's church. Both factors are
evident in this illustration.

> I do not know how to speak of my religious experience in
> the teens. I had gotten along very well without a "religion"
> before, but when I was about fourteen there was a series of
> revival meetings held in the different churches; and going to
> the Methodist church one evening, more out of curiosity than
> anything else, I was so frightened by the evangelist's state-
> ments as to our sinful condition that I became quite excited
> and would probably have "gone forward" if I had not had
> such a decided dislike for the woman who came to urge me to
> "take the deciding step now" and also for the fact that this
> church was neither "father's" nor "mother's church." A week
> later there was another revival, this time in "mother's church,"
> and I let myself be swept off my feet by the enthusiasm for it.
> One noon seven of us girls were going home and saying, "I'll
> go if you will," so that is how I came to "go forward" that
> night. . . . Later on I very much regretted this "conversion,"
> because if I had been let alone until I could think things out
> for myself I would have thought "father's church" the one I
> believed in and really cared for.[57]

Notice above the various contributing factors for this
adolescent conversion. As analyzed, one can see her yielding to emotional needs, group pressure, historical ties, and
inner need. Since adolescence is a time when these factors
seem to be the most effective, it is seen why there have
been more apparent religious conversions in adolescence
than at other times.

Another factor in the adolescent time is that of a sort of
"timeliness," I shall call it. It is here that the youth senses
his place in the history of the reality of living. The older
adolescent begins to look back to the antecedent sources of
the present and think of the future in new terms. This
extension of temporal range, this sense of the past and the

active attempt at deciphering the meaning of the present makes the youth examine his roots. This factor makes adolescence a prime time for any kind of change, including religious conversion. Another factor is the fact that this period of life is one when the youth is an idealist and is preoccupied with utopian reconstructions of society, with a disposition toward the formulation of ideologies. In some this is very pronounced; in others it is delayed or atrophied altogether. Nevertheless it would seem that this would contribute as well to the kinds of decisions religious conversion causes and the kinds of intellectual commitments one makes.[58]

Adolescence is especially significant to the development of moral experience. Morality in its fully developed form is not possible before the time of adolescence if information of Kohlberg and Piaget is significant. First, ethics and morals require a certain degree of intelligence, notably the ability to form concepts and to generalize into categories of thought. Maturity in moral judgment is reached between the ages of seventeen and twenty, according to W. H. Clark.[59] He adds as well that guilt plays a large part in adolescent decision-making. Since the human animal tends to move in the direction that will alleviate guilt and the anxiety that is caused by it, religious conversion has for some a close tie with the alleviation of the sexual guilt emerging in young people.[60] More generalized statements concerning adolescence and religious conversion were made by the early writers. James suggests, for example,

The age is the same, falling usually between fourteen and seventeen. The symptoms are the same—sense of incompleteness and imperfection; brooding, depression, morbid introspection, and sense of sin; anxiety about the hereafter; distress over doubts, and the like. . . . In spontaneous religious awakening, apart from revivalistic examples, and in the ordinary storm and stress and moulting-time of adolescence, we also may meet with mystical experiences, astonishing the subjects by their suddenness, just as in revivalistic conversion. . . . Conversion is in its essence a normal adolescent phenomenon, incidental to the passage from the child's small universe to the wider intellectual and spiritual life of maturity.[61]

Starbuck, on the other hand, saw religious conversion functioning in adolescence as a means of shortening the time of unsurety and of bringing the person out of childhood into the new life of the adult. Conversion would then, for Starbuck, intensify the normal tendencies and shorten the period of storm and stress. And the religious conversion crisis is equated here with identity crisis even though Starbuck was not familiar with the term "identity."[62] Various explanations have been given to explain the reason for so many adolescent conversions. The unique time of adolescence does predispose youth to religious conversion experience in perhaps more quantity than for adults. No one today would hold that conversion is totally adolescent, but certainly adolescence as a developmental factor is influential in religious conversion experience. The period of youth or early adolescence proves to be a time when individuals may be sensitive to the emotions of religious experience. Awe and wonder are more easily expressed, due to lack of inhibition and culture pressure. Pierre Babin has a unique concern for the adolescent's sensitive period as the right time to develop faith.[63] Religious conversion in this period becomes an identity-forming event, " . . . the act or event in which the young person gives his life a direction and meaning in relation to transcendent values, with a depth of consciousness and decision that put an end to the vacillations of his adolescence and profoundly affect the moral and religious sense of his adult life."[64]

The experience being identity forming is unifying at a

deep level, for the experience is defined as at the core of the person. And as Coe suggests in illustrating the feelings of adolescence, there is a vague lack, a general discontent, a feeling of wanting something and wanting to be something that is not clear to one's self.[65] Even though the language used to describe religious conversions' feelings is strong, a sense of incompleteness, a tantalizing awareness of something as belonging to one's true self but not yet realized in one's self, is evident.

Various psychological explanations have ensued to explain the actual occurrence of religious conversion in adolescence. For example, Salzman suggests that it is not difficult to understand why conversion happens in adolescence. It is a period of struggle against authority and an effort to achieve independence which results in hostility. Religious conversion is release of this hostility by joining a group one can agree with.[66] Maloney speaks of regression to the level of infantile trauma in an attempt at some kind of mastery.[67] Stewart related religious conversion with a type of coping exercise wherein the person learns to live in a society where change is expected and not to be feared. And he concludes that there are multiple determinants in the developmental history of each youth that go into making the religious experience of each youth. Not only healthy or sick temperament, or socioeconomic facts, or religious instinct feed into the adolescent idiosyncratic religious complex. He also suggests that the internalizing experience is not isolated to any one age but appears to resolve inner conflicts better following puberty than at any other time. He points up the sex differences in the adolescent experience in showing that in the female the experience may depend upon her passive reactive patterns, her reflection of other's expectations of her and her whole sensory apparatus in a global appropriation of reality. The male uses a more active mode of coping—more identification with the religious figure—Christ, pastor, or priest.[68]

In summary, the developmental context regarding adolescence seems to reflect that this period of time in individual's growth is a time when there is a good possibility of intense change, religious or otherwise. Religious conversion, a type of change, would therefore be more evident in this period.

Whether that change is seen in terms of psychological understandings of "oral" issues related to trauma in early object ties, or whether that religious conversion is explained in terms of coping, the variety of the cause is not as significant as the variety of experience and the commonality of this age period. Whether the conversion is brought about by the change from egocentrality to concern for others, from separation *from* persons to reconciliation *with* them, or from isolation from a community to an allegiance with a new one, religious conversion happens more readily in adolescence due to the sudden handling of emotions, orientation and identity. It has been suggested that it would not be proper to limit the experience to adolescence solely, for along with adolescent concern for change, integration of society with the emerging self-consciousness brings about the opposite characteristics also evident in adolescence, those characteristics such as a time of carelessness, indifference, and doubt. There is also ample evidence of religious conversion at other ages as well.[69]

This, however, is not to say that religious conversion as we have described it does not happen in the teens. The conversion may be more exciting and have with it more accompanying phenomena, or the conflict may be more readily traceable to more normal events of this period of life, but the change is equally as deep as those coming later in life. For adults who have already experienced the trauma of adolescence, religious conversion change may be more traumatic and cause a more extreme unsettling of life. For to be converted may imply to an adult a total change of ideology, and this makes religious conversion less likely, due to the accompanying pressure involved. Certainly the open emotional responses of the teenage years and the ability to establish new allegiances easier than adults are factors in the more common occurrence of this experience in adolescence. Jones goes so far as to state, and I agree, that from the vantage point of today, it seems probable that much of what was called religious conversion in adolescence consisted of conditioned developments expressed in accepted patterns of response, "developments which in contemporary terms might be called identity crises."[70] These crises, brought on perhaps from the extreme idealism of adolescence or the rather traumatic developmental processes involving all of the areas of youth's life, including ideological and emotional commitment, tend to be influential forces for the developmental context of religious conversion. For the religious conversion decision could be an attempt at rationalizing the various forces existing within the youth. It becomes the effective means of releasing the youth from an excessive sense of sin by helping him associate with others who have had the same experience, and through this a sense of community is evolved, giving a sense of fellowship which is equated with "experience." It provides a positive identity, and as Clark suggests, "distracts him from preoccupation with sex by supplying him with a sense of purpose which at its best transcends and includes all other lesser purposes."[71] Thus adolescence is a component relational factor in religious conversion.[72]

It would seem then that the developmental phase of late adolescence and early adulthood has special significance for all subsequent personal change. This is the period in which adult identity takes shape, and it is a time of strong enthusiasm and of a marked tendency toward an emotional polarization. This time is one of great ideological receptivity and of a high experiential intensity. This is not to say that for an adult, religious conversion change will not happen, or to suggest, as Lifton does, that adult change and identity depends upon a specific recapturing of much of the emotional tone which prevailed at the time that this adult identity took shape,[73] but rather that this identity of youth establishes a period of time when a religious conversion experience fits into the kinds of decision-making, maturing, and conflict that is a part of that period. And for an adult to undergo this process, less normal conflict and pressures and tendencies must be evidenced.

PERSONALITY DIFFERENCES

In discussions about religious conversion phenomena the question always arises: Is there one kind of a personality which is more likely to be converted? Are there people who cannot be converted? or "anesthetic" types, as James suggests? In answer to these questions, research has been limited. James suggests that some people, for instance, never are "and possibly never under any circumstances could be converted. Religious ideas cannot become the center of their spititual energy. . . . They are either incapable of imagining the invisible; or else . . . subjects of barrenness and dryness." He also asserts that in some people their inability for religious faith is caused by intellectual problems which check their natural tendencies toward God.[74]

In other persons the trouble is more profound. There are

> men anesthetic on the religious side, deficient in that category of sensibility; just as a bloodless organism can never, in spite of all its goodwill, attain to the reckless "animal spirits" enjoyed by those of sanguine temperament; so the nature which is spiritually barren may admire and envy faith in others, but can never compass the enthusiasm and peace which those who are temperamentally qualified for faith enjoy. All this may, however, turn out to have been a matter of temporary inhibition.[75]

George Albert Coe asked this question more directly and felt free to suggest a possible solution. If, for example, you should expose to a converting influence a subject in whom three factors can unite, such as a pronounced emotional sensibility, a predisposition toward automatisms, and a passive sensibility, Coe felt, you might then safely predict the result: "There would be a sudden conversion, a transformation of the striking kind." With this suggestion Coe asserts the relationship of temperamental factors in the validity of religious conversion, recognizing that this temperamental origin does not diminish the significance of the conversion when it happens, for the ultimate test for Coe is, like James, nothing psychological, nothing definable in terms of how it happens, but something ethical, definable in terms of what the results are.[76] Coe's findings are at least not contradicted by a more recent study by Kildahl (1957, 1965), who found twenty sudden converts in theological schools both slightly less intelligent and somewhat more hysterical than twenty matched gradual awakeners. He hypothesized that the converts would be less intelligent and would perceive authority figures as more threatening. The converts would be more hysterical, undergo more depression, and show fewer humanitarian tendencies. They should be, he felt, more conservative. In his study, the converts went from an admittedly irreligious condition to a religious one. Using various testing materials (the Rorschach, ACE, MMPI, Strong, etc.) he found his group to be less intelligent, scoring higher on the hysteria level of the MMPI, but none of the other hypotheses could be supported. It is interesting to note that in the intelligence scales, the mean scores for both groups fell in the superior range, the 74th percentile for the suddens, and the 87th percentile for the graduals. The hysteria scores were within normal range for the gradual group, with only 4.3 percentile points higher hysteria scores for the sudden group. It would seem that the suggestion that there is a definite personality correlate for sudden religious conversion experience is not successfully demonstrable.[77] Kildahl's groupings were small and may not reflect the average religious convert, but would seem to indicate that students with sudden conversion experiences fall more often into hysteric types on a testing scale and tend to be somewhat less intelligent than their counterparts with a gradual religious development.

James as well suggests that the candidates for conversion are often in the possession of an "active subliminal self" which results in a high degree of hypnotic sensibility.[78] In 1965 Roberts studied some forty-three theological students along several dimensions and found that those who had been converted in the direction of their parent's faith had higher MMPI scores for neuroticism; this was not substantiated in an earlier study by Stanley in 1964, who found a slight negative correlation between sudden religious conversion and neuroticism.[79] A most interesting study done by Wood (1961) and reported by Allison shows that, of twenty-five members of the Pentacostal Holiness religion studied, Pentacostalism attracts uncertain, threat-

ened, inadequately organized persons with strong motivation to reach a state of satisfactory interpersonal relat-
edness and personal integrity. This conclusion, however,
would be tempered by the location of the church (deep
South) and the nature of the cultural and social beliefs
and should not, I believe, be considered sufficient for
general use.[80]

Sargent defines those most likely to be converted in
terms of Pavlov's typology for his dogs, which in turn is
parallel to the Greek typology of the choleric, melancholic,
sanguine, and phlegmatic. The first two types are more
prone to conversion, according to Sargent. Yet Sargent is
quick to indicate that even these types differ within each
group. He notes,

> It is impossible to avoid classifying the human subjects ac-
> cording to basic temperamental types, each of which may call
> for a different type of physiological and psychological treat-
> ment. The stronger the obsessional tendency, for instance, the
> less amenable will the subject be found to some of the ordi-
> nary techniques of conversion; the only hope is to break him
> down by debilitation and prolonged psychological and
> physiological measures to increase suggestibility.[81]

Freudian analysis suggests, on the other hand, that sudden converts tend to have unusually greater repressed resentment and hatred toward their fathers or toward authority in general. This, as observed above (Kildahl), does
not prove out in research analysis; however, most psychologists and psychiatrists believe that for the more regressive
types of religious conversion the personality of the converts is identified by an extreme dependency on strong,
omnipotent figures. And God is the synthesized result of
this need for authority. This may be traceable among those
whose sudden change or gradual shift of center is caused

due to imbalance of pathology or neuropathology, but does not hold true to those of the more progressive type wherein the integration proves to be beneficial to the new believer. It seems obvious that there are individuals who have impaired adaptive capacities, but this has not been established for converts in general.

This problem of a commonality in personality correlates is inconclusive because there is surprisingly little work on this problem. The research is complicated by the previous confusion regarding a definition for religious conversion and by the variety of abrupt and gradual conversion experiences. Possible differences in group conversion and individual ones and the concomitant factors in their occurrences, as well as the very narrow groups studied, further complicate this area.

James, for example, regarded the sick soul as the most likely candidate for religious conversion, for the sick soul is generally introverted and pessimistic in outlook, taking the problems of life profoundly to heart. He seems to be reminiscent of Kierkegaard's man who is in despair and knows he is in this despair. But to attribute sick souls to be the type for religious conversion does not seem to be complete enough. Rather, those who are susceptible to suggestion, those who find pressure and anxiety easily, may find religious conversion the way out. But these will not perhaps be progressive in nature and the experience will not lead them to maturity or identity, but rather be a means of coping, as Stewart suggests, or simply be a form of psychopathological reaction.

The only recurring personality correlate is that of susceptibility to suggestion. Other research seems to be marginal in nature except Kildahl's preliminary work suggesting a slightly lower intelligence and higher hysteria in those with sudden conversions, yet personality as a factor in conversion seems to be rather marginal in conclusion and must be placed rather far down the listing of factors in the experience itself. There is some consensus as to what will prevent religious conversion, however. For example, most authorities agree that it is indifference which best prevents the conversion. A policy of total noncooperation, detachment, and humor seems to be the best defense against induced change, for a lack of involvement avoids commitment. However, this is a will-choice, and not a personality characteristic. It is interesting to note that the choice to not get involved may be the emotional stimulus needed to begin the suggestion of involvement. This paradox is hinted at by Sargent, yet conclusions are not drawn.[82] The opinion that certain personalities are existent in converts proves to be little established, other than be mere speculation or opinion; however, it does seem to suggest that certain types who are more easily swayed by an outside influence may have the occurrence more frequently.

SOCIETAL ADAPTATIONS

Suggestion

Suggestion and suggestibility seem to be factors within the personality that contribute to religious conversion change. However, these are not necessarily thought of as constructs within the personality of the individual, for to be suggestible implies that one is suggestible to some reason or pressure, be it internal or external, conscious or unconscious. Therefore it is important to analyze the contributing factors for this experience to see what goes into the experience itself from outside the person. Suggestion may be caused by sociological and theological influences. When James speaks of outer influences he refers to their effects to the inner life, yet well before the 1900s the role of unconcious mechanisms was clearly appreciated. Coe described the influence of what he called "subconscious automatisms," well-organized sequences of thought or action that in particular circumstances achieve dominance over the conscious, volitional life patterns of man. He thought that conversion could best be understood as a group phenomenon, where the "gang" impulse was operative in temperamentally passive and suggestive people whose nature favored the occurrence of what he called automatisms. He understood the preeminent role of sexual and aggressive feeling in adolescence, but felt that a temporary proclivity was really needed for these problems to be handled in conversion.[83]

Suggestibility is the product of many things. Group pressure, social pressure, style of meeting, concept of belief, intentional manipulation, subtle coercion, and exploitation all lend to suggestibility. There have been discussions regarding, for example, the distinctions between brainwashing and Wesleyan revivalism,[84] with the distinction being made that brainwashing employs intentional manipulation, whereas revival techniques allow for much greater personal freedom and choice. In contrast to this position is Sargent's concern that religious conversions are the direct result of one person or group of people working on others with techniques that are geared to cause the kind of change in behavior or thought patterns that the group desires.[85] An interesting sideline is the research done on sensory deprivation wherein certain trance states and mystical experiences result through sensory overload or denial. This area of research could prove interesting and perhaps aid in the psychological explanation of how the brain functions in these sensorially heavy experiences. It cannot be denied that Sargent's position is demonstrable, and that certain fear arousal or the exhausting techniques of revivalists raise the level of suggestibility. In this state of mind the subject becomes liable for any suggestion from the one suggesting. Hopefully it would not be demonic, yet under these circumstances of complete breakdown as Sargent describes, the person would be vulnerable to even the best or worst intentions. Nevertheless, great and dramatic religious changes occur through these factors.

CULTURE

The experience of religious conversion, a form of deep change and an intense commitment to an ideology— religious in nature—seems to be a common experience of man, exhibited in its varying intensities and lengths. It is conditioned, however, as are any personal experiences, by those things that make man himself, those factors of time, space, culture, society, tradition, place, expectation, genetics, need, and interest. The experience has been suggested as going to the very core of the person and instituting meaningful changes and decisions that are shown in behavior different to that previously exhibited. Yet this experience must be variously understood by the individual within his own time and place. Just as each person is defined by his beliefs, politics, social status, occupation, educational, moral and interest components, so with religious conversion, these factors are also present. Jones suggests that culture is the filter through "which external influences are received and its function as a mold in setting the life style has long been recognized, and this totality also shapes the religious form which, in turn, is part of the very cultural influence."[86] Since conversions of both religious and secular nature occur within culture and take the shape of cultural norms and forms, so the person and his experience are formed by this social, cultural context. He is perhaps even conditioned by it and unavoidably unable to eliminate its power in the religious conversion experience. Take, for example, the effect of the environment on religious conversion. Alland in 1962 in his work on trance state possession, similar in context to conversion, demonstrated how increasing knowledge of the effects of bombardment of the senses alters individual's decision-making faculties. Alland's data are based on observations of the church services of the United House of Prayer for all People, an all-black church founded by C. E. Sweet Daddy Grace. The trance state consisted of a momentary or prolonged loss of voluntary control over body movement, involving mild body convulsions, prolonged dancing, falling to the floor either with body contractions or remaining still as in a faint. He found: (1) a high percentage of carbon dioxide (due to the heat and stuffiness of the room) which can help facilitate mystical-like experiences by enhancement of the ability to see things when the eyes are closed; (2) the loud rhythmic music with a simple repetitious beat; (3) the otherwise forbidden social dancing exempt for the dancing for God in the trance state; (4) the fasting all day by seekers.[87] Accordingly, one sees a selective reduction of certain stimuli with the aim of producing an altered state of experience. The experience here mentioned is often accompanied by glossolalia.[88] Along with the environmental context is the related influence of just general cultural factors.

It has been recognized that in times of general societal unrest, in times of wars, epidemics and the like, more religious conversions can be found. At times of revivals, change in the structure of the group causes certain anxiety in those within the group structure and for those of less adaptive ability, conversion could be a way of rejoining a group or achieving a role change within a group. Boisen related the "Holy Roller" movements during the economic depression of the thirties to similar processes "where the personal conversion experience was a passage right to a group membership."[89] It seems then that religious conversion would not be as likely to occur if the culture or society's traditions did not expect it to occur. This may be the reason de Sanctis' study did not reflect many sudden conversions and why he attributes growth to conversion, solely rejecting sudden instances of conversion in his sample, for the theology of conversion for the Roman Church does not include the usual possibility for the occurrence. Wesley finds this to be the case, perhaps, when he writes: "In London alone I found 652 members of our society who were exceedingly clear in their experience, and whose testimony I could see no reason to doubt. And every one of these (without a single exception) has declared that his deliverance from sin was instantaneous; that the change was wrought in a moment."[90]

It would seem then that the particular form religious conversion effects is the result of suggestion and imitation, which implies that perhaps in other faiths and other countries, although the nature of the change would be the same as in the phenomena here concerned, the occurrences of it would be less or different. James also suggests that in Catholic lands where the sacraments exist as a means of appropriating the holy, the individual need for religious conversion is less stressed and therefore less common. For example, culture imposes certain constraints that tend to offset the natural preference for diversity. "A child brought up in the Confucial tradition could not possibly arrive unaided at the intricate system of Christian theological beliefs."[91] Dewey comments correctly in this respect:

The particular interpretation given to this complex of conditions is not inherent in the experience itself. It is derived from the culture with which a particular person has been imbued. A fatalist will give one name to it; a Christian Scientist another, and the one who rejects all supernatural being still another. The determining factor in the interpretation of the experience is the particular doctrinal apparatus into which a person has been inducted. The emotional deposit connected with prior teaching floods the whole situation.[92]

But it is evident that religious conversion has meaning in various cultural contexts. The fact that in some countries membership in the church or community may be contingent upon having certain experiences indicated that there is for some an expectancy factor evident in religious conversion. It is for some the cultural traditions that bind and form a person into a certain type of belief and therefore shape his experience, and since a man is a being who in many ways works from a stimulus-response reactionism, he may want to move within the context of his tradition or group, society or church, in the most anxiety-free way. He will want to be accepted in the group and culture and it is here that the element of expectation is an important factor.[93]

It is significant to suggest here that religious conversion seems to be group-related in experience. The mystical experience, however, tends to be more singularly related, to be more a core experience. Primarily, as W. H. Clark suggests, the religious conversion experience may trigger a mystical experience but tends to be socially-related, and suggests the mental unifying function of group or crowd control. It seems safe to suggest that emotional tensions are heightened, and the individual's ability to succumb to suggestion is increased when in a social setting where pressures are evident. However, as important as culture and society are, they should not be allowed to totally eclipse the internal coherent system of freedom which is inherent within the person. It is true, of course, that personality is fashioned in and expressed in a social milieu, yet it is a self-contained system as well, as Allport suggests.[94] What may be suggested then is that the cultural influences and social setting in which religious conversion is found or expected are factors in the expression of the experience itself. If required for group membership, the experience occurs more frequently than if it is not required and the social setting therefore seems significant to its occurrence.

REVIVAL CRISIS

A study of religious conversion would not be complete without some reference regarding the social setting of revivalism itself, as this forms for many the cultural context of the experience. Since conversions are most often reported during revivals or immediately succeeding them, the focus of attention in this cultural form must be examined. Revivalism will be here used to mean the attempt at manipulating the environment to produce changes in people. This is not to eliminate genuine revival which is a return to the will of God as perceived by the individual, but rather means the organization of a setting to heighten suggestion and therefore manipulate man to make decisions that he normally would not, a process which induces emotionalism rather than the true emotion which the religious experience truthfully has. The techniques of the professional revivalist have been broadly grouped into the following aims: (1) securing a suggestive audience by the creation of crowd conditions; (2) still further heightening the suggestibility of the audience by raising its emotional tone; (3) securing from the audience the desired response by suggesting the way to respond.[95]

Understood in its simplest terms and psychological elements, the revival is like a process aimed at breaking down previous inhibitions while involving an image of the self as a great sinner. There is an active role that the leader plays in providing the phase of release and self-surrender.

The revivalistic approach is based on the premise that all experience of God is the same and each person must come the same way through the same experience. Realizing that the content of salvation for many churches is the same does not necessarily mean that the method of approach will take the same form. The diversity of people and varieties of experience James talks of so much is denied. There is with this approach a vague relationship or association of fellowship with religious conversion experience. The emotional tone of the revival does not make clear the distinction between these two factors of religious life. Fellowship and its ensuing feeling of closeness, presence, love, and concern are not experience. Fellowship is caused by the situation and promotes an understanding of the application of deep religious change, while religious experience deals in the feeling tones of life and the expression of an understanding of the Holy in the life of man. Fellowship, on the other hand, is created by people and has operating all of the other factors that make community or *koinonia* possible. Revivalism, however, tends to play on uniting the external factors and confusing the experience with the *form* of the experience. The planning and promotion of revival-oriented meetings dates back to Finney, whose *Lectures on Revivals of Religion,* originally published in 1835, is a study of how to sustain pressure, increase guilt, enlarge audiences, and deal with hinderances in the converting process.[96] The Great Awakening in New England was largely the product of Jonathan Edwards who was the first to fully document historically and add a theological defense to what was happening. Much is attributed to Wesley and revivalism. Jones suggests that it was with Wesley that the myth of religious conversion being just sudden occurrences had its formalization and association with revivalism.[97] The rise of revivalism, however, is traced to many causes and not to just the form of the meeting. In the United States population's make up was a factor. Individuals had migrated and now they were without social identity. There was also a new concern about formal religion and a quest for personalization in religion.[98] These factors coupled with the revivalistic approach created a definite kind of spiritual condition, a kind that was not entirely satisfied unless there were some kinds of results. The emotions were stirred to the depths, felt, and decisions demanded.

Many factors bear on religious conversion in this area and on the external forces that cause it. Windermiller showed the relationship of Chinese brainwashing and eighteenth century revivalistic techniques. In his exhaustive study he concludes that there are similarities, such as the crisis experiences and problem-solving processes which aid in stable ego identity; the two processes involve emotional upheaval, bring forth changed lives, and rely on group pressures which involve interrogation, confession, and discussion. They find their similarity in the highly-organized structure and inclusion of new words, exhaustion, suggestion, doubt, fear, and guilt. The results often are the same as well. Yet the two are dissimilar in content, goals, and motivation since they have basically different world views to promote.[99]

Nevertheless, with revivalism came religious conversion. This was due to the format of many revivals. The closing of the meeting was designed to lead up to a time of decision and this was the climax of the crisis drummed up during the meetings. This decision paralleled the giving-in phase of the experience. There is, however, nothing wrong in asking for decisions; prompted times of decision can be meaningful turning points for lives in conflict. But the actual springing of conversion in a sudden and intense way through a procedured, manufactured manner in the hope of acquiring a *quantity* of conversions may be simply environmental factors at work at their best, and the revival technique operating at its fullest potential.[100]

Revivalism then seems to be a factor in the incidence of religious conversion. It contributes to the social situation which in turn affects the individual who encounters the external stress provided. The arousal of fear and anxiety by showing through preaching that man is not all he could be, be it true or false, simply increases the potential for stress and allows for conversion experiences to occur. It is interesting to note here as well that early investigators pointed to these and additional ingredients in the revivalistic atmosphere. Such things additionally mentioned are the concentration of attention on various symbols which arouse emotional images in man, and repetition.[101]

Not only do culture or environmental factors contribute to the incidence of religious conversion. It would seem logical to infer that there might be some social setting that would reintegrate or return to consciousness some early childhood trauma or early religious commitment which would be brought to the fore through the insistence of another person, preacher, leader, or ideology perhaps, which would bring on the emotionalism necessary for an abrupt change or a more gradual one to take place.

Related to this concept are the studies of Carlson who reports on confusional states among college students. These states have a slight relationship with religious conversion in that both tend to have anxiety as a key part of the change process. She states that "some situation recreating the original trauma was the precipitating event for the confusional state, particularly in the conversion experience."[102] It seems reasonable to suggest that there is a similar relationship between the acute initial feelings of anxiety and the situation that perhaps recreates rather vividly memories of past happiness, trauma, or depression and therefore calls back need-fulfilling emotions which in turn give a nudge to the embryonic experience.

On the other hand, in a more gradual religious conversion and shift of allegiance that has definite obvious incubated factors involved, the family plays a large part in the change. Horace Bushnell's concept of nurture is appropriate here, for he feels that sudden conversions in the average family are not too significant and even superficial, and suggested that for the majority of people the long pull of change was most to be preferred. He attributes to "ostrich nurture" the expectancy factor in religious conversions by adding:

Again there is another and different way in which parents, meaning to be Christian, fall into the ostrich nurture without being at all aware of it. They believe in what are called revivals of religion, and have a great opinion of them as being, in a very special sense, the converting times of the gospel. They bring up their children, therefore, not for conversion exactly, but, what is less dogmatic and formal, for the converting times.... To bring up a family for revivals of religion requires, alas! about the smallest possible amount of consistency and Christian assiduity.... So they fall into a key of expectation that permits, for the present, modes of life and conduct which they cannot quite approve.... Finally the hoped for day arrives, and there begins to be a remarkable and strange piety in the house. . . . The children stare, of course, not knowing what strange thing has come! They cannot be unaffected; perhaps they seem to be converted, perhaps not.[103]

For Bushnell, nurture toward conversion was hard, involving truly total involvement by the parents each day, and was closely related to the biblical concept of sanctification. Religious conversion for Bushnell could be caused by too many external factors and these kept him eternally critical of conversion of the sudden variety. These factors, such as the family, the early childhood experiences, and expectation of the revivalistic approach seem to be additional factors in the occurrence of the experience of conversion.

PSYCHOLOGICAL GROWTH

In understanding the contributing factors in the crisis of religious conversion, some time must be spent dealing with the psychological factors in the process itself, at least those theorized as being operant in conversion. Some of these processes have been alluded to previously, but what follows is additional material regarding some contributing factors in the dynamics of the experience. Some theories only suggest intelligent speculation, others based on research tend to show more reliably the factors involved.

Understandings of the psychological nature of religious conversion vary. Sargent, previously cited, alluded to the positive correlation between modern psychoanalytic and psychiatric interpretations which see conversion as psychologically like the process of self-abnegation, which leads to brainwashing. In his discussion he traces the many uses of the psychological mechanisms which recondition the individual by causing intense anxiety and strong emotions such as anger, fear, hate, and guilt. This process wipes the "mind clean and allows new concepts to be instituted."[104] Irving Rinder has studied the same process in the area of role change when one self-role is substituted for another through the application of debasement or processes of degradation, according to Furgeson.[105]

Main explanations of the dynamics of religious conversion deal with the concept of the ego. Christensen suggests that all religious conversions are simply attempts at a reintegration of the ego's defense systems, some of which succeed and some which do not.[106] In this description of dynamics the ego then, in a process of symbolic conscious representation, acts on the unconscious conflict and the suppressed conscious conflict seeking out a solution. When the solution comes, there is a sense of well-being, elation, and understanding. Since the ego is not integrated with the conflict there would be a normal sense of completeness of the self. But to the believer the experience is attributed to happening outside of the self.

Those who deal with the pathological implications of this kind of rapid change see in religious conversion a successful attempt at solving problems, real or imagined. If the conflict would not be resolved positively and maturely in a religious conversion experience, there might be a retreat into schizophrenia or schizoid states as the magical solution to the problems. This regression type of religious conversion would occur when the inner struggle with authority, independence, hostility, and resentment becomes too great for the normal ego's defensive network and there is a break. In order to explain the positive integration factors of unity and behavior that often accompany a conversion, individuals of this bent simply apply Freud's understandings of "regression in the service of the ego" which always has a positive outcome aiding maturity.[107] Oftentimes religious conversion is related to personality reorganization. Boisen felt this way and differentiated between those which lead to maturation and positive results and those which end in some kind of psychosis. Salzman and Sullivan's early paper ("Schizophrenia: Its Conservative and Malignant Features") suggests that some sort of pathology is responsible for the experience itself. It seems reasonable to assert then that conversion under this framework would result in a unification of the personality on a socially unacceptable basis, rather than on an acceptable one. If psychosis and conversion were alike in their source, then the cataclysmic eruptions of acute psychosis and conversion would be nature's attempts to eliminate the sets and attitudes that hamper growth and effect a reorganization of pathology. The difference then between someone being a gifted and dedicated Christian convert or a backward schizophrenic would be the fact that they were predetermined by the character elements which they brought into the crisis of conversion.[108] But to prove this is another problem and has not yet been scientifically done. For the present this must remain a theory.

In addition to those who see conversion as a psychopathological situation can be added those who, rather than theorize concerning the nature of the experience, suggest the psychological dynamics involved. For example, religious conversion could be then the interpretation of paired changes in the level of ego-functioning. This occurs first in the form of regression followed closely by a sudden reintegration. It is like other regressions before release, but the reintegration usually is long-lasting. It seems that moving into the area of the dynamics of conversion is more profitable, for in looking at its psychological functioning one does not have to theorize as to the nature of the source, be it pathology or normality. Again Carlson's work on confusional states is helpful here. She suggests that religiosity may be one of the outcomes of the confusional states of youth, and therefore religious conversion reflects normal reaction formation and dissonance theory.

Much of psychoanalysis attributes religious conversion to the realm of simple attempts to handle repressed material seeking consciousness which are within the framework of religious beliefs. It is logical that Freud's theories would then reflect an attempt in conversion to resolve the Oedipal conflict.

Other research ties religious conversion to brain functioning. After lobotomy operations, when the mind is freed from its old straitjacket and new beliefs take the place of the old ones, experiences similar to religious conversions take place. These are directly man-oriented and are simply surgical attempts at organization within the conflict model.[109]

More recently, those studies on sensory deprivation and its resultant effects on behavior and change seem significant. A series of studies done by Solomon (1961) have altered the usual patterning of sensory experience by preventing physical movement, blocking vision, hearing, and touch. Under such conditions there appears an hallucinatory-like activity.[110] This observation has led to some speculation as to the relationship of sensory deprivation to mental illness. For the social deprivation of the psychotic could be then creating a situation of perceptual isolation likened to the laboratory experiments. It would be well for further study to be given to this area of mind functioning. For a study of the circumstances under which changes occur, whether in a group or in isolation, with sensory overloads and stimuli present, or in formation regarding the patterning caused by groups and environment may yield a rich information regarding the actual process of change within the perception of the convert.

On the whole, however, most seem to agree that there are actual processes of the mind that are operant in the change, if not the cause itself. James's concept of "subconscious incubation," for example, is simply the current concept of repression by which that which is unhappy, painful, or incompatible in the mind of man and in his consciousness is banished into a region called the unsconscious from which it may influence behavior or conscious processes of thought but cannot be voluntarily made a part of the conscious stream of thought. Whether one wants to attribute the dynamics of religious conversion to the realm of the conscious, the unconscious, or as Jung would, the beyond-individual-consciousness forces of the collective unconscious and its concomitant archetypes in exerting pressure for personal integration or disintegration within the individual, is up to the particular school of psychoanalytic thought one wishes to embrace. Since man is a multiplicity of motives, energies, relationships, and yet unique, most of these ego functions as well as the popular vocabularies of change could apply under given situations and given enough observational time. Whether one wishes to adopt the concept that the dynamics involved are simply regression in the service of the ego, repression, abreaction, or sense deprivation, is not the issue so much as the fact that there are various psychological functions occurring, dynamically resulting in change. As mentioned earlier, whether or not the divine is operant in these changes is not without possibility or even probability but certainly could be included as a valid additional factor if one wanted to take the position that religious conversion is a deep kind of change when properly understood. The sudden kinds of religious conversion easily may be seen to have dynamics psychologically oriented and operating, due to their observational nature. They may have regressive or progressive outcomes but the change may be just as deep and devastating in reorganizing and in redirecting the life of the individual toward new goals and in giving new motives grounds for being.

It seems then that both the theologians and the psychologists were to a degree right concerning religious conversion—the theologians claiming it as a positive phenomenon, and the psychologists assuming that there very well could be some pathology present in some cases. Both positions acknowledge the actual fact of this kind of deep change. Both positions realize the complexity of isolating a locus for change within the person. The pressure on the early writers of religious conversion, such as James, Starbuck, Leuba, et al. to take a stand on the issue of conversion forced them to make perhaps the best stand and conclusions regarding it. Starbuck says: "The ultimate test doubtless will be, does (conversion) contribute, in the long run, in the individual and in groups of individuals, to permanent growth?" The settlement of such a question far exceeds the maturity of the psychology of religion.[111]

It would seem then that an outline could be made as to the dynamics involved in religious conversion, as well as to the contributory contexts of the experience. Illustration 2 is a compilation of this sort. In it is included those elements that make up the dynamics and factors in the experience. It is to be noted that the illustration is not intended to be complete, nor does it show relational factors. Rather, it is used to illustrate the various factors in the conversion process attested to in the foregoing chapter and is to be used

THE CONTEXT OF CONVERSION

Illustration 2: The following illustrates the interrelationships of the various contexts which form the fabric of conversion experience.

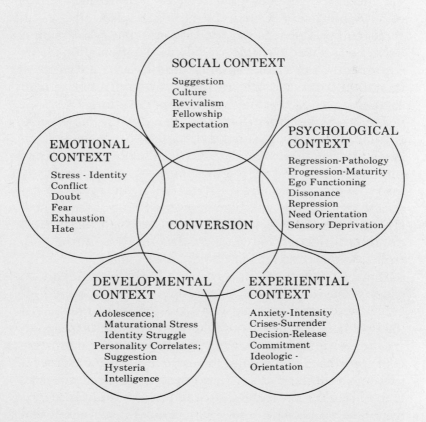

SOCIAL CONTEXT

Suggestion
Culture
Revivalism
Fellowship
Expectation

PSYCHOLOGICAL CONTEXT

Regression-Pathology
Progression-Maturity
Ego Functioning
Dissonance
Repression
Need Orientation
Sensory Deprivation

EMOTIONAL CONTEXT

Stress - Identity
Conflict
Doubt
Fear
Exhaustion
Hate

CONVERSION

DEVELOPMENTAL CONTEXT

Adolescence;
    Maturational Stress
    Identity Struggle
Personality Correlates;
    Suggestion
    Hysteria
    Intelligence

EXPERIENTIAL CONTEXT

Anxiety-Intensity
Crises-Surrender
Decision-Release
Commitment
Ideologic -
    Orientation

as a guide and paradigm of the totality of the experience. The fabric of religious conversion is attributed to these elements, and the organization of the circles shows the fact that each element is related. None can be seen in isolation completely. Just as the emotional fabric of the religious conversion experience may be affected by the developmental context, so can the experiential feel be attributed to the social and psychological context. The relationship is one of intermixture, and the elements must be seen in their totality, isolated only as one particular conversion is examined. If, for example, the ideologic orientation of the convert is to a particular understanding of God, it must be seen in the context of the group or developmental stage of the person in order for it to be properly understood.

The various factors that institute a change may be organized, emphasized, and even suggested, but the process of the change itself seems to be beyond any type of manipulation and control. Psychological attempts at controlling the process do not seem to be significant in themselves; rather the conditions are what are controlled. Change occurs from within. There seems to me to be a definite distinction between the factors that can be controlled and the process of change itself.

It would appear that the process of religious conversion is a movement toward wholeness and integration, and includes a decision to deal with the onrushing realities of living. These realities may be from an ideological, theological, social, developmental, experiential realm, but are perceived as real and needing resolution. The fact that integration occurs around a core event, an event that gives meaning to the future as well as to the past and present, is important. It becomes a new way of looking at oneself and at life, and the crisis function aids in this integration and direction. The decision gives direction, usually in a theological sense. Its content is usually that of Christian tradition. The return to God at the core. In this sense, religious conversion is in its deepest sense a decision involving the appropriation of an "Other," the Christ figure. In Christian tradition conversion marks the beginning of the process of living the Christian life, however perceived, and because decision is an act which occurs in a period of time, it seems sudden, yet as shown may be incubated through conscious or unconscious elements. And as mentioned, in times of crises men make major decisions, if only because of the nature of crisis itself. For it is in these times that fate, as it were, is hanging on the line. "Crisis periods have therefore creative possibilities," suggests Boisen. They are periods of change and they make or break a person.[112] They are crisis in a positive sense, a chance for change.

Another context of religious conversion is this concern with "I." The ego concerns of conversion are significant. The life centers in on such topics as existence, values, traditions, right and wrong, sin, life itself, culture, meaning and direction—problems whose resolution seem momentous for the person. The direction and result of the conversion experience is centered in a new identity, the identity of a group, person, tradition, ideology, or movement. But it provides a place where one fits as well as an ego identity, which will be discussed at length in the following chapter.

The positive results of conversion (those inner-experienced), such as security, happiness, resolve, and direction, to say nothing of the observed completness expressed by converts, seem to indicate the uniting effect of religious conversion. The inner sense of unity is due to the feeling emotions of these experiences themselves, as well as to the new unity of ideology that accompanies the decision. The content in the ideology may not necessarily be complete, only fragmented, in the beginning, but conversion's movement toward completion tends toward ideological frameworks as well.

Before a more detailed analysis of the relationship with identity experience itself it is necessary to move from religious conversion into the equally fascinating experience labeled "identity." At this point the reader needs to be reminded of the aims of this book. We wish not only to see the function of the conversion experience, but to see what relationship this has with identity formation and crisis. As can be seen, the topic of conversion is gigantic, and the reader is encouraged to proceed to follow some of the footnoted material for an in-depth study of this phenomenon. Those factors that have a relationship with identity have been stressed; the functional elements as well as some causal contexts have been suggested. Further development of this relationship must wait till proper understanding of the identity experiences is attained. Then the relationships will be drawn. Nevertheless at this point it seems reasonable to insist that this profound change called religious conversion is a realignment of interests and attitudes containing beliefs, commitments, values, and resulting in changed behavior. The process is never complete, for man is always in movement, yet it brings an intense change affecting man where he is most affected, at the center of his being, at the core of his life.

We leave religious conversion then for the time being, only to return in summary and conclusions as relationships are drawn. We pause now for an understanding of the concepts of identity as they bear on this experience—religious conversion.

NOTES

1. Carl W. Christensen, "Religious Conversion in Adolescence," *Pastoral Psychology*, XVI (September, 1965), p. 21.

2. William James, *The Varieties of Religious Experience,* Mentor Books (New York: New American Library of World Literature, Inc., 1958), p. 192, suggests that the believers in the nonnatural character of sudden religious conversion admit that class plays little part in conversion experience. "The supernormal incidents, such as voices and visions and overpowering impressions of the meaning of suddenly presented scripture texts, the melting emotions and tumultuous affections connected with the crisis of change, may all come by way of nature, or worse still, be counterfeited by Satan. The real witness of the Spirit to the second birth is to be found only in the disposition of the genuine child of God, the permanently patient heart, the love of self-eradicated." Thus, the experience or the natural causes or even effects are not a test of conversion's validity.

Ellen G. White adds, *The Great Controversy* (Mountain View, California: Pacific Press, 1888), p. 473,

> Popular revivals are too often carried by appeals to the imagination, by exciting the emotions, by gratifying the love for what is new and startling. Converts thus gained have little desire to listen to Bible truth, little interest in the testimony of prophets and apostles. Unless a religious service has something of a sensational character, it has no attraction for them. A message which appeals to unimpassioned reason awakens no response. The plain warnings of God's word, relating directly to their eternal interests, are unheeded ... (in) truly converted ... the relation to God and to eternal things will be the great topic of life." Leon Salzman in "Types of Religious Conversion," *Pastoral Psychology*, XVII (1966), p. 12, lists two kinds of conversion—the progressive type ". . . only in the sense that the movement is forward in terms of personality development, permitting greater maturity. . . . This conversion could be called a conjunctive one, brought about by a lessening of

anxiety; it is the integrating maturing development in the life of the person . . . equivalent to the 'Aha' experience, . . . insight . . . the experience of *satori* arrived at in Eastern religions." Another type of conversion he calls regressive where pathology is operant in the experience.

3. John C. Lilley, *The Center of the Cyclone: An Autobiography of Inner Space,* (New York: Julian Press, Inc., 1972), pp. 6–23.

4. George Albert Coe, *The Spiritual Life* (New York: Eaton & Mains, 1900), p. 51.

5. E. D. Starbuck, *The Psychology of Religion* (New York: Charles Scribner's Sons, 1915), p. 155.

6. H. R. Bagwell, "Abrupt Religious Conversion Experience," *Journal of Religion and Health,* VIII (April, 1969), p. 164–165.

7. Robert H. Thouless, *An Introduction to the Psychology of Religion* (Cambridge: Cambridge University Press, 1971), p. 104.

8. Paul E. Johnson, *Psychology of Religion* (Nashville: Abingdon Press, 1959), p. 127.

9. Starbuck, *Psychology of Religion,* p. 94, table XI.

10. Leon Salzman, "Types of Religious Conversion," *Pastoral Psychology,* XVII (1966), p. 17.

11. James, *Religious Experience,* p. 195.

12. Christensen, "Religious Conversion in Adolescence," p. 26.

13. William J. Samarin, "Glossolalia," *Psychology Today* (August, 1972), p. 79.

14. Johnson, *Psychology of Religion,* p. 127.

15. James, *Religious Experience,* p. 171.

16. Christensen, "Religious Conversion in Adolescence," p. 26.

17. James, *Religious Experience,* p. 171.

18. See Lewis Sherrill, *The Struggle for the Soul* (New York: Macmillan Co., 1955), pp. 25–40 for a significant contribution to the relationship of crisis to growth within the Christian life.

19. Barbara Eleanor Jones, "Conversion: An Examination of the Myth of Human Change" (Ph.D. dissertation, Columbia University, 1969), p. 249.

20. George Barton Cutten, *The Psychological Phenomena of Christianity* (New York: Charles Scribner's Sons, 1908), p. 241. It is also interesting that theologian Seward Hiltner, "Toward a Theology of Conversion in the Light of Psychology," *Pastoral Psychology,* XVII (1966), p. 38, suggests a cognitive element in

any type of conviction. Using the Alcoholics Anonymous experience of conversion, equally dramatic or gradual, he lists the following cognitive factors in their change: "(1) accurate understanding of the immediate enemy from which deliverance has been won; (2) social support that transcends one's natural psychological defenses; (3) a discipline which is not prevented by pride from looking ever and again at the source of deliverance, and which is aware that it has been saved in 'principle' rather than 'all over.' This is, in truth, a spelling out of what Martin Luther meant by saying that the redeemed man in Christ is *simuliustus et peccator.*"

21. James, *Religious Experience,* p. 164.

22. Ibid., p. 198.

23. Paul Tillich, *The New Being* (New York: Charles Scribner's Sons, 1955), p. 116.

24. See Robert Jay Lifton, *Thought Reform and the Psychology of Totalism: A Study of "Brainwashing" in China* (New York: W. W. Norton & Co., 1956), p. 49; Barbara E. Jones, "The Myth of Human Change," p. 254; or J. D. Frank, *Persuasion and Healing* (Baltimore: John Hopkins Press, 1961), for a discussion of healing power.

25. Starbuck, *Psychology of Religion,* p. 128, table XVI.

26. H. M. Tiebout, "Conversion as a Psychological Phenomenon in the Treatment of the Alcoholic: Therapeutic Mechanisms of Alcoholics," *The American Journal of Psychiatry* (January, 1944), p. 469.

27. James, *Religious Experience,* p. 186.

28. Christensen, "Religious Conversion in Adolescence," p. 17.

29. Starbuck, *The Psychology of Religion,* p. 94, table XI.

30. Clarence Augustine Beckwith, "Conversion," *The New Schaff-Herzog Encyclopedia of Religious Knowledge,* 1963, III, p. 263.

31. James, *Religious Experience,* pp. 169-170.

32. Ibid., p. 203.

33. Walter Houston Clark, "Intense Religious Experience," *Research on Religious Development: A Comprehensive Handbook,* ed. by Merton Strommen (New York: Hawthorne Books, Inc., 1971), p. 533.

34. Robert E. Mogar, "Current Status and Future Trends in Psychedelic (LSD) Research," *Journal of Humanistic Psychology,* V, No. 2 (Fall, 1965), p. 161, in his research regarding change and

drug use, suggests that the work dealing with crisis-experiences like Erikson concludes that the personal crisis is not pathological but a critical choice point in life demanding a leap of faith which may become the catalyst for an emerging inner conviction or awareness and forthcoming change.

35. James, *Religious Experience,* p. 201.

36. See Frederick Morgan Davenport, *Primitive Traits in Religious Revivals: A Study in Mental and Social Evolution* (New York: Macmillan Co., 1905) for an example of this.

37. Frank, *Persuasion and Healing,* p. 112.

38. Thouless, *Introduction,* p. 104.

39. Leon Salzman, "The Psychology of Regressive Religious Conversions," *Journal of Pastoral Care,* VIII, No. 2 (1954), p. 75.

40. William Sargent, *Battle for the Mind* (New York: Harper & Row, 1957), p. 144.

41. Ibid., p. 143.

42. Vergilius Ferm, ed., *Puritan Sage: Collected Writings of Jonathan Edwards* (New York: Library Publishers, 1953), p. 374.

43. Christensen, "Religious Conversion in Adolescence," pp. 19, 20.

44. Leon Salzman illustrates this belief in "Types of Religious Conversion," p. 18. He remembered in 1936 a meeting in Canada in which a preacher spent an entire sermon attacking the faculty of a seminary; "They were unfit, not Christians, and so on," and ended the sermon with a call. A number responded and were presumed converted. The dynamics of the call were hate, he suggests, and appealed to similar feelings in the ones who responded.

45. See Ibid. and also see a brief discussion of witchcraft in "Witchcraft," *The Oxford Dictionary of the Christian Church,* ed. by F. L. Cross (London: Oxford University Press, 1958), p. 1472. Also included is enumerations and chronological outbreaks of witchcraft and the ensuing reformations within the Christian Church.

46. For a good study of the revivalism of early America, the cultural, personal factors in its early and rapid rise, see William Warren Sweet, *Revivialism in America: Its Origin, Growth and Influence* (New York: Abingdon Press, 1944).

47. G. Stanley Hall; William James, *Religious Experience,* p. 162 ff.; George A. Coe, *The Spiritual Life,* pp. 29–55, where he

discusses the mental state of adolescence and the religious feelings of youth; Paul Johnson, *Psychology of Religion*, pp. 81–97 adds an especially good section on the religious development of adolescents; see also Charles W. Stewart, *Adolescent Religion: A Developmental Study of the Religion of Youth* (Nashville: Abingdon Press, 1967).

48. James Bissett Pratt, *The Religious Consciousness: A Psychological Study* (New York: Macmillan Co., 1926), p. 122.

49. Clark, "Intense Religious Experience," p. 532.

50. American Institute of Public Opinion, Press Release, April 15, 1962.

51. Robert J. Havighurst and Barry Keating, "The Religion of Youth," in *Research on Religious Development: A Comprehensive Handbook*, ed. by Merton P. Strommen (New York: Hawthorne Books, Inc., 1971), p. 690.

52. Charles William Stewart, "The Religious Experience of Two Adolescent Girls," *Pastoral Psychology* (September, 1966), p. 49.

53. Arnold Gesell, *Youth, The Years from 19 to 16* (New York: Harper, 1956), p. 336.

54. Robert J. Havighurst, *Human Development and Education* (New York: Longmans, Green & Co., 1953), pp. 9–41. Adapted from Part I.

55. Ronald Goldman, *Readiness for Religion: A Basis for Developmental Religious Education* (New York: Seabury Press, 1965), pp. 161–162.

56. M. H. Podd, "Ego Identity Status and Morality: An Empirical Investigation of Two Developmental Concepts" (unpublished Ph.D. dissertation, University of Chicago, 1969), quoted in Lawrence Kohlberg and Carol Gilligan, "The Adolescent as a Philosopher: The Discovery of the Self in a Postconventional World," *Daedalus: Journal of the American Academy of Arts and Sciences* (Fall, 1971), pp. 1051–1086.

57. Luella Cole, *Psychology of Adolescence* (New York: Rinehart & Company, Inc., 1948), p. 370.

58. A more detailed study of the contributing factors in identity development will be in the following chapter.

59. Walter Houston Clark, *The Psychology of Religion* (New York: Macmillan Co., 1958), p. 122.

60. Ibid., p. 117.

61. James, *Religious Experience*, p. 164.
62. Starbuck, *The Psychology of Religion*, pp. 224, 262.
63. Pierre Babin, *Faith and the Adolescent* (New York: Herder and Herder, 1964), pp. 111–115 suggests that sensitive period be used to mean the stage in which the subject is inclined to a particular attainment "by virtue of a maturation of the function necessary for this attainment. Thus during childhood there is a period sensitive to learning to speak."
64. Ibid., p. 122.
65. Coe, *Spiritual Life*, p. 50.
66. Leon Salzman, "Types of Religious Conversion," p. 19.
67. James C. Maloney, "Mother, God and Super-ego," *Journal of the American Psychiatric Association* (1954), p. 120.
68. Charles William Stewart, "The Religious Experience of Two Adolescent Girls," *Pastoral Psychology*, XVII (September, 1966), p. 54.
69. See ibid. Recent studies indicate that among some revivalistically-oriented groups the age of conversion is dropping from the teens down into late childhood (See D. Yoder, *Nurture and Evangelism of Children* (Scotdale Pa.: Herald Press, 1959); Robert O. Ferm, *The Psychology of Christian Conversion* (Westwood, N.J.: Fleming H. Revell Co., 1959). Ferm believes the ripe age to be higher and points out that by using college students as their subjects, many of the early studies unwittingly were operating with a truncated sample. In surveys of three churches, Ferm found the average age of conversion to be 43, 46, and 41 years respectively. Converts made by Graham's first British campaign averaged in their middle thirties. Carl G. Jung, in "The Psychological Foundations of Belief in Spirits," *The Structure and Dynamics of the Psyche*, Bollingen Series, Vol. XX (New York: Pantheon Books, 1960), pp. 301–318 emphasized mid- to late-thirties as a period of moving from an extroverted, external reality mastery orientation, while Hiltner ("Theology of Conversion," pp. 35–42) writes that conversion is most important, likely, and easily cultivated in the thirties rather than in the early teens.
70. Jones, "The Myth of Human Change," p. 211.
71. Clark, *Psychology of Religion*, p. 117.
72. Christensen delineates the component parts of conversion that relate directly to adolescence ("Religious Conversion in

Adolescence," pp. 27, 28). (1) There are predisposing factors of a specific unconscious conflict plus the adolescent age; (2) there is a conscious conflict related to the unconscious conflict which produces guilt, anxiety, and depression; (3) there is an acute reaction which is precipitated by intensification of the foregoing through participation in a religious meeting; (4) there is withdrawal from others because of a new sense of estrangement and a feeling of unreality; (5) there are feelings of submission which follow in the surrender phase with a sudden understanding and feeling of elation accompanied by auditory and visual events; and (6) this change modifies his behavior. The analysis is only generally relative, for the factors that cause conversion are only dealt with in the first two stages, those being conflict and its results.

73. Lifton, *Thought Reform,* p. 469.
74. James, *Religious Experience,* p. 167.
75. Ibid., p. 168.
76. Coe, *The Spiritual Life,* p. 144.
77. John P. Kildahl, "The Personalities of Sudden Religious Converts," *Pastoral Psychology,* XVI (September, 1965), p. 37.
78. James, *Religious Experience,* p. 193.
79. Clark, "Intense Religious Experience," p. 532.
80. Joel Allison, "Recent Empirical Studies of Religious Conversion Experiences," *Pastoral Psychology,* XVII, No. 8166 (September, 1966), p. 26.
81. Sargent, *Battle for the Mind,* p. 137.
82. Ibid., pp. 107–110, 225–233.
83. Coe, *The Spiritual Life,* p. 128ff.
84. See below, n. 88.
85. Sargent, *Battle for the Mind,* pp. 200ff.
86. See Jones, "Myth of Human Change," p. 155.
87. Allison, "Empirical Studies," p. 26.
88. Allison, (ibid., p. 29) also quotes a study by Stone (1963) of a community in the gulf states whose membership was contingent on conversion signaled by a vision. In the narratives of the vision, all the elements of classic conversion were present including primary feelings of being lost or disorganized, self-surrender, and feelings of newness, but the crux lies in the attainment of a vision with definite visual symbols given by God to signify his promise for future help. For final acceptance into

membership the vision is made public with the accompanying high emotionalism of crying, marching, and shouting. Stone reported that the religious visions occurred mostly during adolescence and there was considerable backsliding after visions. The content of the visions also contained material personally and culturally related to these people.

89. Anton J. Boisen, "Economic Distress and Religious Experience—A Study of the Holy Rollers," *Psychiatry* (February, 1939), p. 185.

90. James, *Religious Experience*, p. 184.

91. Gordon W. Allport, *The Individual and His Religion: A Psychological Interpretation* (New York: Macmillan Co., 1950), p. 23-24.

92. John Dewey, *A Common Faith* (New Haven, Conn.: Yale University Press, 1940), p. 12.

93. It is on this concern that James Bissett Pratt, *The Psychology of Religious Belief* (New York: Macmillan Co., 1907), p. 153 comments, "the violence of the experience is in part induced by the suggestions of conventional theology and in part is purely imaginary, existing in the expression rather than in experience. I venture . . . at least nine out of every ten conversion cases reported in recent questionnaires would have had no violent or depressing experiences to report had not the individuals in question been brought up in a church or community which taught them to look for it if not to cultivate it."

94. Gordon Allport, *Pattern and Growth in Personality* (New York: Holt, Rinehart & Winston, 1963), X-XI.

95. Alfred Clair Underwood, *Conversion: Christian and Non-Christian: A Comparative and Psychological Study* (New York: Macmillan Co., 1925), p. 202.

96. Charles G. Finney, *Lectures on Revivals of Religion,* ed. by William G. McLoughlin (Cambridge, Mass.: Belknap Press of Harvard University Press, 1960), pp. 91-120.

97. Jones, "The Myth of Human Change," p. 168.

98. William Warren Sweet, *Revivalism in America: Its Origin, Growth, and Influence* (Nashville, Tenn.: Abingdon Press, 1944), pp. 3-22.

99. Allison, "Empirical Studies," p. 30.

100. No attempt has been made to historically outline and chronologically set apart revivals in history. For more formal

discussions of revivalism's impact and approach see Sweet, *Revivalism in America*.

101. See Ames, *The Psychology of Religious Experience*, p. 330; Coe, *The Spiritual Life*, p. 146; John W. Drakeford, *Psychology in Search of a Soul* (Nashville, Tenn.: Broadman Press, 1964), pp. 195–196; and Hadley Cantril, *The Psychology of Social Movements* (New York: John Wiley and Son, Inc., 1941), pp. 64ff.

102. Helen B. Carlson, "The Relationship of the Acute Confusional State of Ego Development," *International Journal of Psychiatry*, XLV (1961), p. 517.

103. Horace Bushnell, *Christian Nurture* (New Haven, Conn.: Yale University Press, 1888), pp. 62–64.

104. Sargent, *Battle for the Mind*, pp. 150ff.

105. Earl Furgeson, "The Definition of Religious Conversion," *Pastoral Psychology*, XVI (September, 1965), p. 10.

106. Christensen, "Religious Conversion in Adolescence," p. 25.

107. See Joel Allison, "Empirical Studies," pp. 122ff. and Charles William Stewart, *Adolescent Religion*, pp. 266ff. for a more complete analysis of this process.

108. Bagwell, "Abrupt Religious Conversion Experiences," p. 168.

109. Sargent, *Battle for the Mind*, p. 139.

110. Philip Solomon et al., *Sensory Deprivation: A Symposium Held at Harvard Medical School* (Cambridge, Mass.: Harvard University Press, 1961).

111. Starbuck, *The Psychology of Religion*, p. 164.

112. Anton Boisen, *Religion in Crisis and Custom: A Sociological and Psychological Study* (New York: Harper & Brothers Publishers, 1945), pp. 68–69.

CHAPTER IV

IDENTITY: The Way to Become

"I walked out to the hill just now. It is exalting, delicious, to stand embraced by the shadows of a friendly tree with the wind tugging at your coat tail and the heavens hailing your heart, to gaze and glory and give oneself again to God—what more could a man ask? Oh, the fullness, pleasure, sheer excitement of knowing God on earth! I care not if I never raise my voice again for Him, if only I may love Him, please Him. Mayhap in mercy He will give me a host of children that I may lead them through the vast star fields to explore His delicacies Whose finger ends set them to burning. But if not, if only I may see Him, touch His garments, and smile into His eyes—ah then, not stars nor children shall matter, only Himself." Elisabeth Elliot.

Social science suggests a term which has relevance to those interested in the religious realm. The concept "identity" has been broadly understood. It has been used so much in the past decade it is in new need of refinement. The Americans, the Africans, the clergy—yes, even the Telephone Company—can have an identity crisis. According to a most eloquent spokesman for this concept, Erik Erikson, so can Martin Luther or Gandhi.

We have seen the varied use of this return to God— conversion. We have seen the interaction of its psychosocial elements. Key to this understanding is the self-integration of the conversion experience itself. The by-product of the experience, this response-by-return to God is the knowledge, even self-authenticating knowledge of belonging again to the kingdom of God.

> Praise be to the God and Father of our Lord Jesus Christ who has bestowed on us in Christ every spiritual blessing in the heavenly realms. In Christ He chose us before the world was founded, to be dedicated, to be without blemish in His sight, to be full of love; and He destined us—such as His will and pleasure—to be accepted as His sons through Jesus Christ, in order that the glory of His gracious gift, so graciously bestowed on us and His Beloved, might resound to His praise.[1]

This positive concept of fitting and finding a place in the family of God and in the world, this commitment and resolution of personal conflict in returning to God in conversion, this becoming one of God's own children finds a close friend in the psychosocial phenomenon of identity.

The problem is, however, that the term "identity" has many meanings and it follows as well that there are as many theories from which concepts of identity are derived. David De LeVita suggests that, "Conceptual meanings that are valid only at a certain level of complexity may be used erroneously on other levels."[2] Since a concept like identity touches so many fields of study, clarity in definition is helpful, even though apparently difficult, since identity is presented as a conceptual framework that links the individual and his culture so closely together.

Sorting out the various definitions of identity and then using their essence or commonalities for extrapolation to the religious conversion experience is difficult, since our concern is more about the experience of personal identity than theories of identity. Only brief treatment of identity theory is necessary. Among the many ideas extant for discussion regarding personal identity are these: the ability to know and experience oneself as having continuity (Eissler); the apparent satisfaction one finds in achieving and playing a role (McCall and Simmons); the idea of separateness from life (Kramer); the interaction of one's view of himself with that of the perception of others (Greenacre); a deep belief in how one fits in the scheme of life (Wheelis); knowledge and experience of an almost mystic true self (Kramer and Wheelis). There are others who use personal identity to simply mean the role one plays (Strauss). Identity can as well be represented by more than seventeen different connotations or focal points.[3]

Writing from an entirely different background than many of those mentioned, Erik Erikson gives us a most detailed framework for identity formation. Although he deals with conversion and its relationship with identity only briefly in his books *Young Man Luther* and *Gandhi's Truth,* his concepts allow for extrapolation to the conversion experience itself.[4] One aim of this book is to do just such a relational observation.

An understanding of the term "identity" must be specifically established. Thus far, the term "identity" has meant in a commonsense way, "knowing where one fits." This definition is not as specific as it could be. It does, however, emphasize the experience of personal identity. As social psychologists use "identity," you sense a sort of organizing concept which is ambiguous and diffuse and almost as elusive as the feelings of personal identity.[5] For the social psychologists, identity is seen usually as a product of interaction with others in social settings. When we move into its literal derivative sense, that of equal sameness, we move out of the realm of a concept in consciousness to its usage in math and logic.

Looking at the history of this term, as does De LeVita,

we see its roots in logic as really a controversial paradox in logic. Our interest is in its relationship to people. We are interested not in logic's relationship, but "namely the identity of the human personality, this being the history of the concept of person itself."[6] This person concept has Old Testament roots. Who people really are becomes the biblical identity question. Exodus 34:33–34 suggests that Moses put a veil over his face, a mask, so to speak, when communicating with the people, but when in contact with God, he took it (the mask) off.[7] What is implied is the direct confrontation with the Creator God; all false roles and non-me identities must be shunned. It is here we have a unique touchstone with conversion experience. In relationship with God, all false identities are gone. Real-knowing-who-I-am identity is demanded for a change to take place. To build new roles, one must be free of false gods and false roles. In God, or "in Christ" in the Christian tradition or Pauline sense, we find the real knowing-who-I-am-me.

Understanding identity takes us from the science of logic and math through Locke to Hume. But it is interesting to note that a shift takes place during these times, a shift from its roots in the concepts of epistemology ("How do I know that a frog is the same as a tadpole in essence and not form, and therefore has a common identity?") to a more psychological concept, a consciousness approach with psychological, even metaphysical, overtones. For example, "I know I have a common Jewishness that transcends my time and space and role in life"—a personal identity, an idea of consciousness and continuity and fit and belonging. For some, William James is seen as the progenitor of this latter understanding.

James saw the concept of identity helpful in determining his definition. First, he uses that concept of identity which is laid down in the proof of who we are. This substantialist view includes such things which are determinators of our personal identity: name, profession, physical attributes. Secondly, James would reason out one's identity by association. "I call the same things mine because they arouse the same feelings in me." This sense of one's things arousing in us a sense of possession not found in things which are not ours locates personal identity in the conscious sensation, almost physical sensation of owning something. James's third sense is purely transcendental. If you want something to possess identity, James would suggest, it is possessed a priori by the ego.[8]

Erik Erikson added to this a psychosocial quality in identity's development. For Erikson, the term "identity" finds its roots in Freud. The term itself cannot be primarily attributed to Freud, however. Since Erikson claims a rich relationship with many of Freud's teachings, it does not seem inappropriate that Erikson's usage is clouded with Freudian overtones. When referring to his link with the Jewish people, Freud referred to an "identity" which aimed attention at the rich blending of the values and culture which were his heritage.[9] Erikson is quick to pick up on this concept uniting something in the core of the person with something that is central to the cohesion of the group. He suggests,

> The young individual must learn to be most himself where he means most to others—through others, to be sure, who have come to mean most to him. The term expresses such a mutual relation in that it connotes both a persistent sameness within oneself (self-sameness) and in a persistent sharing of some kind of central character with others.[10]

When Erikson talks of identity, he stresses the psychosocial forces extant in personal development which recognize the importance of society and culture on personality formation. A second important aspect of identity is that person himself. Thus, Erikson stresses ego functions in identity. He mentions the series of conflicts that confront an individual as he copes with prescribed tasks in society. These conflicts occur in time, age, and are resolved in the person. Therefore, to understand identity one must take into account the mutual interaction between the individual and the society in which he finds himself.[11] There is this dual nature for identity, then. He defines it as being a maintaining of continuity of the self and identifying at the same time with something beyond oneself to acquire the essential characteristics of the group to which one belongs.

Erikson, in illustrating identity, builds on William James as an example. "A man's character is discernable in the mental or moral attitude in which, when it came upon him, he felt himself most deeply and intensively active and alive. At such moments there is a voice inside which speaks and says, 'This is the real me.'"[12] Erikson suggests that James uses "character" to describe his term "identity." Identity, for Erikson, however, must be prefaced with the term "a sense of" for this better describes the feeling tones of the experience itself. In defining identity, we are dealing with a process at work within man, a process located "at the core" of the individual, and yet also "at the core" of human culture, a process which establishes, in fact, the identity of those two identities.[13] Identity is therefore usually coupled with the noun "formation" which stresses the processional aspect of it. The formation of identity employs a process of reflection and observation which takes place at all levels of mental functioning, "by which the individual judges himself in the light of what he perceives to be the way in which others judge him in comparison to themselves and to a typology significant to them; while he judges their way of judging him in the light of how he perceives himself in comparison to them and to types that have become relevant to him."[14] Erikson claims that this process is for the most part unconscious except where inner conditions and outer circumstances combine to aggravate a painful or elated identity consciousness.

Moving beyond this dual quality of identity, Erikson tries not to define identity too narrowly and sees various connotations for the term itself. There is a conscious sense of individual identity, of striving for some kind of continuity within the personal being. Identity also provides a criteria for the "silent doings of ego-syntheses" and proves a means to provide inner solidarity within a group's ideals and larger identity. Erikson admits that these connotations may be ambiguous to some, but he insists that they do help to circumscribe the problem of identity.[15]

Erikson stresses the dynamic process which is identity. For example, it is not the maintenance of a system the individual has ordered within himself; rather, identity makes possible the maintenance of certain essential features of an individual, as well as his society, because the ego is responsible for the continuity of self that began in infancy and remains open to current identification and role change through life. Erikson calls this continuity, this drive for sameness, this congruity at the core of person, ego identity. The identity takes on the nature of a governor for change and is implicit within forces of change for the person.

This sense of personal sameness is what K. R. Eissler developed with his contribution to identity understanding. He suggested that the "self" is an independent structure inside of personality. Since not all areas of one's self are accessible for investigation, the assumption seems logical.

Identity then becomes the feelings of experiencing one's self as a continuum; while Rapaport and Jacobson argued against Eissler's concept when first proposed, still Eissler's concept of a sense of knowing when one is right with one's self and a continuous, real self transcending one's personality carries on James's and Erikson's consciousness approach.[16] At the same time, identity takes on a sense of continuity and integration. We see identity being defined as a sense which involves some relationship with others and personal perception of one's place alongside others and their action with others.[17] While agreeing with this, Soddy adds that identity always has an anchorage in a social matrix.[18] Even Berger and Luckmann see the dialectic between people and their world bringing out one's identity. They occasionally slip into this consciousness concept as seeing personal identity anchored "in a cosmic reality protected from both the contingencies of socialization and the malevolent self-transformation of marginal experiences."[19] It is to some major proponents of personal identity in this latter sense that we now turn.

Hans J. Mol in his book *Identity and the Sacred* explores the relationship of identity to religion. In defining identity, a discussion of the various foci of identity appears. Mol would place identity in a continuum with personal identity on the left, moving to group identity mid-stream, while social identity represents the far right, criticizing any approach which defines identity by excluding the interaction of group and social identity with one's own personal identity. He suggests:

Personal and social identity very much depend on one another, but there are also numerous possibilities for conflict between the two. Even so, conflict is only one of many reasons for the fragility of the frame of identity. Death, diffidence, conquest, economic disasters, injustice, and, in modern societies, an excessive emphasis on instrumental values, relativization and over-choice of identity foci are some of these reasons.[20]

It is personal identity which most closely correlates with the self-integration of religious conversion or return. Mol, however, who seems to see the whole continuum of identity related in forming one's real identity, would use "boundaries" to define the factors influencing identity and giving it meaning. Identity, on the personal level, becomes that "stable niche" man finds himself in amid the chaos of a world and environment. The stable nature of this niche (identity) is what man must defend. As the boundaries deteriorate, so does the definition for personal identity. Similarly, on the social level, "a stable aggregate of basic and commonly held beliefs, patterns and values maintains itself over against the potential threat of its environment and its members."[21] And identity is again defined by its expected limits out of which the sameness and continuity is destroyed. This emphasis on personal identity, with focus on clearly-defined, expected boundaries, gives insight into the nature of religious expectations placed by one's life or community.

Mol's insistence to move beyond clearly-defined expectations and roles, which are the product of social expectations, to a more stable, conscious level for identity, moves him to believe that identity is more enduring than a galaxy of roles and phases of maturity.[22]

Identity, then, means selfhood, "anchored in a transcendent order symbolized in concepts and myths: less self-conscious than taken-for-granted."[23] This stable niche in the whole interchanging complex of interaction is the feeling of identity. One problem with Mol's understanding of identity is that when we blend the identity experience with the religious experience of identity, namely conversion, as we have seen, we find that religion, and specifically the experience of conversion, does exactly what Mol's understanding of identity does. Conversion return is a major source of stability and strength, and possesses roles and social mores which provide one's identity itself. His definition as that stable niche leads us nicely into seeing conversion as a major identity-forming experience which is one by-product of religious commitment. Mol, as does De LeVita, likes more sympathy for those who think of identity as "the most essential nucleus of man which becomes visible only after all his roles have been laid aside."[24] It is in this light that Mol can assume that identity defines what a person, group, or society really is. He contrasts this objective designation with morality, which emphasizes more what a group or person does than what a group or person really is. Identity, then, is that which gives meaning to existence and that experience which interprets life itself.

Mol's emphasis on the unique fabric of meaning as identity is in contrast to those who see identity in all these areas—personal, social, and groups—as being related to "whatever in the social environment provides the individual members of a society with his or her identity."[25] Identity transcends, in an almost *superadditum* way, and becomes that which gives a person, society, or group its own unique wholeness; yet groups and societies, yes, even religion, attempt through manipulation and suggestion, coercion and explanation of "truth" to form and pattern and locate individuals' identities. It is in this subtle interplay between the patterning of something in religion and the ability of individuals to perceive personal identity, that identity really emerges, and as Mol suggests, the individual is often the enemy in this process because he senses a uniqueness and a wholeness which he sees in himself beyond the patterning which is given him in the society, group, or even himself.[26]

IDENTITY: COHERENT SENSE OF SELF

Allen Wheelis depends upon phenomenal self-theory and sees identity as a coherent sense of self. He suggests that the sense of self is deficient now. Adolescents' quest for answers to probing questions of "Who am I?" and "Where am I going?" gets no sufficient answers any longer. Finding the coherence within oneself is a challenge facing us all. For Wheelis, the group provides the stability in this world of shifting patterns.[27] Coming from a psychoanalytical background, or as he claims, "from behind the couch," he sees personal identity in a slightly different context than does Mol. Personal identity for Wheelis is "dependent upon the awareness that one's endeavors and one's life make sense, that they are meaningful in the context in which life is lived."[28] Personal identity for Wheelis relies on some type of stable value system which is consummate with the conviction that one's values and actions are harmoniously related. Coupled, then, with the sense of wholeness and continuity that a value system provides is the fact that with a value system one knows how to choose and then how to act. In the interactions with others, in the absence of dissonance between belief and practice, one's personal identity emerges and is experienced. True personal identity then becomes a creation out of living in congruity with one's values, values which are given and lived by one's own groups or even, say, religion. For Wheelis, identity is linked correctly with values. It is found specifically "on those values which are at the top of the hierarchy—the beliefs, faiths, and ideals which integrate and determine subordinate values."[29]

Personality for Wheelis is seen growing and reshaping with each new value and action. Personal identity in this sense is not finding something that had been lost. Personal identity and its sense of presence in the life is created and achieved in this value matrix. "Values determine goals, and goals define identity," claims Wheelis.[30] If this is the case, as Wheelis suggests, the return in conversion to God and the ideological value framework which religion provides becomes an identity function for the emerging self, since personal identity of Wheelis's variety sees personal identity as socially being formed through instrumentalities which have continuity.

Wheelis quickly cautions us, however, about his view for fear that we would overstate religion's function as putting excess emphasis on values in identity formation. He suggests that we may be guilty here of mixing levels of theories and generalizations, rather than looking specifically at structure or existence.[31]

A firm sense of personal identity provides in a most poetic way both "a compass to determine one's course in life and ballast to keep one steady. So equipped and provisioned, one can safely ignore much of the buffeting. Without such protection more vigilance is needed; each vicissitude, inner and outer, must be defined and watched."[32] Return to God in this deep sense of commitment, which religious conversion provides, finds close anchorage in Wheelis's theory.

IDENTITY: THE MIRRORS OF OTHERS

Personal identity is approached by Anselm Strauss as deriving from "judgments of others, and a particular brand of mask or identity is fashioned by an anticipation of these judgments."[33] This position, which stresses the role of identity one finds with interaction with others has been seen as a fundamental identity context in others, including Mol, McCall, and Simmons, as well as in Greenacre.

Through the evaluations, appraisals, and judgments of others, and by our own judging of ourselves, we mirror the identity expected. Often the role of others is seen as an important factor in becoming what we perceive ourselves to be. Ministers in training during their first parish experience often find this personal identity totally determined by their expectations and the role models given by the members. The pastor arrives, little expecting himself to be what others think he is, but as the demand comes to be the interior decorator, financial wizard, parish priest, prophet, and king, his once weak, personal role identification becomes strong. Implicit roles defined by his parish begin to be incorporated into his life. The incompetent pastor, now believing that he is an authority in the church in areas such as decorating and finance, almost ignores the doctrine of the priesthood of all believers and begins to demythologize it. Later on in his ministry, these roles, having been reinforced down through the years, show their impact on the pastor's own personal identity.[34]

Strauss suggests that "the masks he then and thereafter presents to the world and its citizens are fashioned upon his anticipation of their judgments. The others present themselves, too; they wear their own brands of masks and they are appraised in turn. It is all a little like the experience of a small boy first seeing himself at rest and posing in the multiple mirrors of the barber shop."[35]

Religion could play a major role in establishing personal identity, then, especially organized and rigidly structured institutionalizations of religion. A religious sect proposes what will happen as you encounter another in a religious interchange. If it happens, the religious forecasting is validated and the learner has mastered the prescribed steps. His identity within the religious group is already ordered for him by the group's identity validation or as Strauss says: "Kneel, knight, and receive knighthood." These graduation points, these turning points in one's growth within an institution program identity.

With this instrumental function, personal identity is related to the place of group think and group expectations which become prominent. Certainly others help shape one's vision of personal identity, but identity is the basic sense of congruity rather than mimicking roles. For Strauss, then, fantasy and daydream become important functions in personal identity formation. Through them you must guess what might happen in the encounter and what the expectations might be. One must evaluate the important encounters which have high risk for change. They may even be rehearsed ahead of time, Strauss would suggest. It is much like a movie director rehearsing his scene.[36]

The touchstone of this emphasis of personal identity formation makes change come when the risk is minimized. Religious conversional identity, however, reflects Strauss's implications only when the God one perceives or sees revealed sends a vision of how it best might be to belong to him. Yet included in relational identity formation for Strauss is a sense in which personal identity is the congruity and continuum of one's nature itself. In clarifying this concept, Strauss uses an amusing illustration.

> We have before us an uncooked egg. We may choose to boil, scramble, or poach it, or make it into a dozen different kinds of omelets. Regardless of the treatment this egg receives, it remains an egg. Some people like their eggs hard, some soft, and some very finicky eaters draw fewer specifications. To the extent that any claim is made that "This egg is not cooked," all

this can mean is that in more or less degree the egg is finished. Up to the point it becomes converted into charcoal and is really finished, the cooking of the egg represents a matter really of degree: no matter how the egg changes in appearance, it is still essentially an egg.[37]

This quality of eggness Strauss would perhaps call ego identity, rather than personal identity, for identity comes basically in the fateful appraisals of others by ourselves.

Other contributors to identity theory add little beyond those already mentioned, save Erikson whose formation theories will be explicated in detail next. Bellah's suggestion that personal identity is a statement of what a person or a group is, seems vague. De LeVita focuses on the "formants" of personal identity, namely the body, name, and life history, all of which come together to provide one's real self. Yet these individuals provide little additional information to the concept of personal identity.

Probably the greatest contributor to identity formation is Erik Erikson. His work already briefly cited moves personal identity from just a discussion of one's authentic self or simply discussions about the importance of others or roles in identifying one's personal identity to a detailed discussion of the actual formation in the sense of identity. His life-cycle concerns relate so directly to our discussion of religious conversion experience and the change it brings that more detailed exposition is warranted before we can discuss the relationships of how religious conversion and identity theory interact with religion and theology and biblical concepts of personhood.

IDENTITY: THE CYCLE OF LIFE

Erikson links the identity crises of youth with specific events in psychosocial history. He does, however, make a unique distinction in definition. Personal identity and ego identity are separated for Erikson and are often found attached to his usage of the term "identity." I find Erikson using these terms rather loosely, which I believe is surely logical, for he is defining a process rather than an object. He usually is referring to the term "ego identity" when he speaks about identity. Personal identity involves the simultaneous perception of one's self-sameness and continuity in time, the mere fact of existing, where ego identity refers to the ego quality of this experience.[38] The simplest definition offered by Erikson is that ego identity is an answer to the questions "who am I and where am I going?" Yet the complexity of identity formation requires a larger and more exacting answer. Ego identity for Erikson is "the awareness of the fact that there is a self sameness and continuity to the ego's synthesizing methods, to the style of one's individuality, and this style coincides with the sameness and continuity of one's meaning for significant others in the immediate community.[39]

Identity is closely tied to an understanding of the stages of man. Erikson sees eight in all. These stages represent crises that each person has in the process of developing an ego identity. But ego identity itself represents the cumulative product of a person's completion of the first five stages of development prior to and including late adolescence. The first four stages, occurring in infancy and childhood, are characterized by a series of conflicts or crises, as Erikson calls them. Identity is the result of the successful resolution of these stages of crises. In the mastery of each stage and with successful resolution of the crisis in each, certain moorings for identity emerge. In summary, the early crises center in infancy, around the development of trust or mistrust; during childhood, the establishment of autonomy vs. doubt and shame; during the preschool age, the emergence of initiative or feelings of guilt; later in the school age, the appearance of industry or feelings of inferiority; and finally at adolescence, the struggle between identity and role diffusion becomes central for the person.[40]

To denote the area of conflict, the term "crisis" is used by Erikson. For him it is a "moment of decision between strong contending forces."[41] The crisis that may ensue may happen rapidly; various viewpoints and options may become isolated. Thus the phrase "identity crisis" can be defined in Eriksonian language as a moment of decision between forces pulling for a positive identity and forces suggesting a negative identity or identity diffusion.[42] Identity defined thus as a process finds itself always changing and developing. "At its best it is a process of increasing differentiation, and becomes ever more inclusive as the individual grows aware of a widening circle of others significant to him. . . ."[43] It is a process that begins in the first true meeting of the mother and baby as recognition takes place, yet has its normative crisis in adolescence. Identity has its roots in what went before and in many ways is the decisive event which determines what goes on after.

While defining identity, Erikson is careful to keep a close association with the crisis in the individual and the contemporary crisis in historical context. Each crisis helps to define the other; their relationship is one of mutuality. Erikson spends a great deal of time in *Young Man Luther* on just this point.[44]

Erikson, the psychoanalyst, finds himself critical of his own methodology in asserting that one cannot really grasp the term identity within the psychoanalytic method, for it has not developed terms to really understand the environment.[45] This phenomenological viewpoint makes Erikson's intermixing of environment and development most significant and his concept of identity so inclusive. His emphasis on the psychosocial nature of identity, this stress on the interpersonal relationships which mark out the self, are equally aspects of it. Erikson calls identity the personality organization framed through the feedback from others.[46] Note then that the process of identity is dynamic, as its definition is itself. It is not static maintenance of a system the individual has organized within himself; rather it is, despite strong forces aiding change, the process that makes possible the maintenance of certain essential features of an individual and his society. This continuity of self-representation is ego identity, and its development is neither passive nor static.[47]

Erikson's major contribution is in his epigenetic principle and identity formation. He postulates that every growing animal has a ground plan of organization from which the parts emerge, each part emerging at its time of special ascendancy until a unified whole is produced. Yet in addition to this inner urge for development, there is social growth and familial growth operating as factors in the developing. This implies a kind of psychic determinism in that each psychic event is determined by those which precede it.[48]

His methodology has been helpful in the construction of the human life cycle. Various factors are being validated on the cycle itself which make his conceptualization more valid. For example, in *this* study, conversion is seen as validating identity crisis and thus making his scheme in this area acceptable in theory. Erikson is careful not to place absolutes on his diagram of the life cycle of man. Identity does not have an age, for it is a process, beginning in infancy, finding meaning in adolescence or late adolescence, and striving to be validated in a period of time at the very end of life called "beyond identity." Erikson does not assign ages, as does Piaget, to his cycle, and he is like Goldman in allowing variations within the cycle. The scheme then is a broad picture of how life is lived, and his observations, even though clinically colored through extremes in observation, nevertheless are enlightening for consideration and investigation.

Integral to an understanding of identity for Erikson is his delineation of the life cycle, with its significant eight stages of development. Before attention can be specifically drawn to the most crucial stages for this study—that of identity vs. identity diffusion—a brief overview of the other stages is in order to fully understand the general outlook of Erikson's approach. The life cycle has been alluded to as a major premise for Erikson's work.

Basic to the life cycle is the *epigenetic principle*. This principle suggests that in each living thing there is a pattern which must unfold, with the various parts emerging, each with a time of special ascendancy, until a functioning whole is formed. Yet the cycle of life is not an isolated entity. Erikson really speaks of two cycles in one—the cycle of one generation concluding itself in the next and the cycle of the individual life coming to its own conclusion. This concept reflects the dual nature of identity as well.[49]

Living together in the cycle of life is more than just a physical proximity alone. It means that the individual's life stages are "interliving," cogwheeling with the stages of other people. This cogwheeling moves man along as he interacts with their life stages. Erikson, in speaking of the life cycle, states "I have, therefore, in recent years attempted to delineate the whole life cycle as an integrated psychosocial phenomenon, instead of following what (in analogy to teleology) may be called the 'originological' approach; that is, the attempt to derive the meaning of development primarily from a reconstruction of the infant's beginnings."[50] This aspect of involving other elements to affect the development of the person in addition to the past growth problems is a significant contribution to developmental approaches.

Erikson suggests that it is well for all to remember this epigenetic principle—anything that grows has a ground plan—and that each item of the vital personality to be analyzed is related to all the other aspects, each depending on the proper development in the proper sequence of each item. Another principle for Erikson is that *each item exists in some form or another* before its time of ascendancy. He illustrates this principle by suggesting that a sense of basic trust is the first component of healthy mental vitality, the first virtue to be established in life, and comes in the first crisis of life. It is the encounter with the stages of Erikson and their resulting crises which are important for healthy identity; a positive or nearly positive solution to them is important for healthy identity to be formed. Each successive step then is a potential crisis. (Crisis for Erikson is not a crucial threat of catastrophe, but must be viewed as a turning point, a crucial period "of increased vulnerability and generational strength and maladjustment.")[51]

These stages are not the only factors causing conflict in a person, for they must be understood in the context of time and in the framework of the social influences and traditional institutions which determine perspectives on the infantile past and on the adult future.[52] Thus a person moves from one stage to another as soon as he is able, biologically, psychologically and socially.

Each of the stages of the psychosocial crisis is balanced by *alternative attitudes*—one positive, the other negative. Erikson uses the word "versus" (vs.) to indicate the person's struggle between the two polarities and also to indicate the intensity of their polarities. When facing one of these crises in the stages of the cycle, man is responsible for its resolution. He can go either way, positively or negatively resolving it. If the positive attitudes outweigh the negative ones, the individual is moving toward a healthy mental viewpoint; yet he may not, and probably will not, solve the crisis totally on the positive side. These crises and their positive resolution should be viewed as the framework for a healthy ego. The healthy ego develops when the crises are settled positively, and an unhealthy ego develops when the crises are settled negatively.

Erikson emphasizes that first each component of the healthy personality is "systematically related to all others," and that they all depend on the "proper development in the proper sequence" of each criterion; and secondly, that each component "exists in some form before 'its decisive and critical time" normally comes.[53]

As previously noted, the ego's role in this process of stages is that of regulator and guide. It can give a feeling of sameness in the midst of the crisis and therefore, like identity, finds its function as that of assimilator of media, stimuli, and society, much as conversion functions. Erikson's cycle is closely related to the developmental scheme in that he finds within these stages a phase-specific task that must be solved. His theory defends the concept that *the ego is integrally related to the process of identity formation.*

Erikson warns against the misuse of the cyclic theory, cautioning that there are many who would make a sort of lock-step approach to the stages, a stage approach to check on the maturity of youth and adult. The nature of the cycle approach is one of unfolding and reunfolding, and those who view it in a rigid way ignore the fact that the ego in the healthy person must continually reconquer the negative aspects as they crop up in the life.

It is proposed that by understanding the eight stages of man, one would understand a great deal about man's life.

By understanding the crises he encounters and noticing the successive conflict resolutions in his life, we would learn a great deal about man's later life. Erikson's centering in on the psychosocial development of man does not exclude his interest in other kinds of development, such as sexual, cognitive, etc. But he points out that the psychosocial development is a process of conflict and crisis resolution where the other forms of development may very well not be.

It would seem, then, that there are four major insights Erikson provides in relationship to religious conversion: 1) The theory of epigenesis of the ego or the gradual opening up of the process of the personality of an individual; 2) a theory of social relationships important to healthy growth, whereby the individual as he develops incorporates the culture and time-space realities to form his own reality and development; 3) a concept of crisis whereby the person systematically reaches resolutions which verify his identity and aid the process of identity; and 4) a concept of ego development wherein identity experiences become an integrative force for the totality of the person and are experienced in crisis with resultant effects.

Since identity proceeds in this cycle of life, the first crisis is very important. Identity for Erikson is formed in a resolution of trust versus mistrust. The basic psychological attitude to be learned at this stage is that "you can trust in the world in the form of your mother, that she will come back and feed you, that she will feed you the right thing in the right quantity at the right time, and that when you're uncomfortable she will come and make you comfortable, and so on."[54] By basic trust Erikson means that there is some sort of correspondence between your needs and the world. Yet to learn to mistrust is just as important. There is, for

Erikson, a certain ratio of trust and mistrust in our basic social attitude that is critical. When we enter a new situation we not only are able to trust, but we must know how much to mistrust as well.[55]

Erikson postulates some virtues that are evolved through this state. Hope is vital for the survival of a people for a healthy identity and is a basic human strength without which one could not exist. In man, hope is established through the lifelong struggle begun in childhood between trusting and mistrusting, and through these crises hope is reaffirmed throughout life.

Once established, hope is a basic quality of experience and is evidenced for Erikson in the enduring belief "in the attainability of fervent wishes, in spite of the dark urges and rages which mark the beginning of existence. Hope is the ontogenetic basis of faith and is nourished by the adult faith which pervades patterns of care."[56] It is this quality in identity faith that I believe is directly related to conversion experience. Conversion experience itself produces in a very abstract sense the possibility for the Christian to see beyond where he is now and vision where he might be.

The sense of trust is established more often by the mothering one, and this qualitative maternal relationship formed the basis for a sense of identity which will later combine a sense of being "all right," of being oneself, and of becoming what other people trust one will become. A significant suggestion by Erikson is that there are various social institutions that correspond to the stages he postulates. For the first stage, religion is the corresponding institution. It is religion that synthesizes and socializes the deep crises of life. It is conversion which best confronts these crises, and through return to God resolves them. Mistrust is the source of evil; and religious traditions and rituals provide a collective restitution of basic trust, which in the mature adult becomes a combination of faith and realism.[57] At this early stage of childhood development, early formation of identity, the child, having learned to trust his mother and the world to some extent needs to become self-willed and take chances with the trust that he has learned. He must see what he is; he must experiment with his will against others to develop in this stage. Autonomy seems to result from the successful resolution of feelings of shame and doubt that show up during this age. Erikson would illustrate this shame and doubt by saying, "This is the age when the child begins to blush, which is symptom of knowing one is being watched (from the inside, too), and is found wanting."[58] An individual who has not resolved this conflict and cannot be autonomous will act inferior all of his life. Through successful resolution of this conflict, he will constantly encounter that feeling. There is in each crisis a ratio to be found. Neither positive or negative is eliminated entirely. This stage comes into prominence during the second and third years of life, according to Erikson.[59]

The two organ modes which correspond to the second stage are those of retention and elimination which begin to function alternately, not only to the sphincters, but also with regard to all functioning aspects of the child. They teach the child the social modalities of "holding on and letting go." Just as sense of trust and mistrust is related to the parental existence of guidance and faith, so is autonomy a mirror of parental dignity. Erikson advises parents with a child in the first stages to be firm, tolerant, and yet gentle with him, so he will learn to be the same himself.[60]

The social institution in this stage is the principle of law and order. Erikson suggests the young child should be able to reflect on the dignity and the lawful independence of

his parents. Parents who are not able to function autono-
mously because of the societal pressures cannot be expected to build autonomy in their children.

The virtue or ego strength Erikson attributes to this
stage is that of will.

> *Will, therefore, is the unbroken determination to exercise choice as well
> as self-restraint, in spite of the unavoidable experience of shame and
> doubt in infancy.* Will is the basis for the acceptance of law and
> necessity, and it is rooted in the judiciousness of parents
> guided by the spirit of law.[61] (Italics his.)

During this stage the child must yield to the wills of new
individuals he meets. He must run the risk of yielding.
Erikson says that is it the task of judicious parents to honor
the privileges of those who are strong in will and still to
protect the fact that the weak have rights. This stage will
gradually grant a measure of self-control to the child who
learns to control willfulness. "To offer willingness, and to
exchange goodwill. But in the end, the self-image of the
child will prove to have been split in the way in which a
man is apt to remain split for the rest of his life."[62]

In the third state—locomotor-genital—the Oedipal situation is common and the process of identifying with a strong
parental figure is accepted. Erikson adds to this concept
the idea that the child is now seeing what kind of a person he may become. The crisis in this stage is brought
about by three developments: 1) the child is learning to
move freely and violently within the society and has a
larger radius of goals presented before him; 2) his cognitive skills are emerging and providing him a greater language ability and comprehensive scope; and 3) with the
first two developments the child has an enlarged imagination and can visualize roles beyond his comprehension.
Out of this must emerge, according to Erikson, a sense of

initiative as a basis for a realistic sense of ambition and purpose.[63] The major organ mode for this stage is classified "intrusive." This includes intrusion by physical attack, aggressive talking, intrusion into the environment by locomotion, and a never-ending curiosity. The social mode for this stage is that of "being on the make," and includes the joy of competition, goal-making, and conquest. The social influences now begin to be a part of the context of growth, and an exemplary basic family is important for the child to successfully see initiative established. The society provides identity prototypes that take on meaning in this stage.

The ego strength which evolves is labeled "purpose." It is the "courage to envisage and pursue valued goals uninhibited by the defeat of infantile fantasies, by guilt and by the foiling fear of punishment."[64] It is through the medium of play that the child develops purpose, for infantile play is a trial universe where the past is enacted and projected on a larger and more perfect future stage. This is a time when marriage and family loyalties are important for it is in these that the conscience of the child finds unity and direction.

This stage appears in the fourth and fifth years of a child's development. He attempts to resolve the conflict of a sense of initiative and of guilt for not being himself. Here is manifested the mode of intrusion and inclusion aided by ideal societal prototypes. Ego strength and a developing sense of purpose are most treasured at this stage.

School age provides new tasks with which to identify. A sense of industry is contrasted with inferiority. Since the child has previously had time to play, he now sees a sense of industry in his purposeful responses. The danger of this stage is that he will develop from himself and from his task the "well-known *sense of inferiority*."[65]

Feelings of inferiority are developed from a sense of

being inadequate because of a lack of technical ability. The child feels he is deemed useless by society.

There are no organ modes for this stage or any succeeding stage. Society meets the need for the child to make things by providing some instruction (school) so the child can learn and master the basic skills of his society's technology. Since this stage involves making things, creativity must be stressed, and it is here that Erikson first notes a danger in this stage of identity development.

> If the overly conforming child accepts work as the only criterion of worthwhileness, sacrificing imagination and playfulness too readily, he may become ready to submit to what Marx called "craftidiocy," i.e., become a slave of his technology and its dominant role typology. Here we are already in the midst of identity problems, for with the establishment of a firm initial relationship to the world of skills and tools and to those who teach and share them, and with the advent of puberty, childhood proper comes to an end.... School age ... identity can be expressed in the words "I am what I can learn to make work."[66]

For man, this is the end of the identity development. The experience itself provides enough sense of congruity to establish the technocrat in a comfortable identity.

The virtue for this stage is that of "competence." This is related to task fulfillment due to certain specific skills. It is the "free exercise of dexterity and intelligence in the completion of tasks, unimpaired by infantile inferiority."[67] This stage then emerges in the elementary school years, brings a sense of industry while avoiding a sense of inferiority, manifests the social modality of making things, and is joined by the instruction provided by skilled others to develop competence as the child's ego strength.

The identity stage is one which we must study more

closely, for it offers a major contribution to religious conversion's experience.

With the advent of puberty as a context for identity, the struggle between a sense of identity and a sense of identity diffusion seems to develop, only to reach its major crisis in late adolescence. Since Erikson defines identity in terms of ego strength, which is the confidence that one can maintain inner sameness and continuity and is reinforced by the same understanding about oneself by others, identity then is a primary task of this age. The opposite of this would be a sense of diffusion, a syndrome which appears when one is unable to maintain the inner sameness, and according to Erikson, especially in accordance with an occupational identity. In general it is the inability to settle on an occupational identity that is most troubling to youth. Those who do not find identity tend to find the resolution to the crisis in diffusion or a negative identity. This is Erikson's explanation of Luther's refuge in the monastery, for example.[68]

The social institution which Erikson claims is the guardian of identity is ideology. This concept is not just a system of beliefs, but also includes the concept that people will promote what is the best for others. The youth must convince himself that those who succeed in their adult worlds are responsible for promoting what is the best. Erikson suggests that it is through these ideologies that the "fiber of the next generation is found. . . . Adolescence is thus a vital regenerator in the process of social evolution."[69] The social modality for this stage is that of "being oneself, or not being oneself" and of "sharing being oneself." It is seen that identity concern is the chief problem here.[70] It is here that the moratorium needs to be provided by society for the youth to reflect without pressure and to feel out ideological, emotional, and identity relating options. The moratorium concept could be a meaningful methodology for the religious educator and perhaps provide for more gradual growth in spiritual things rather than for the acute, crisis-type changes that conversion often exhibits.

The ego strength which emerges with adolescence is fidelity, which is "the ability to sustain loyalties freely pledged in spite of the inevitable contradictions of value systems."[71] Fidelity for Erikson is the cornerstone of identity and becomes important through the process of conforming ideologies and affirming companions. There is a great deal of societal context in this age for identity to be confirmed and for it to be an important factor in the developing person.

As identity is formed the person faces its ascendance in the adolescent years and through them attempts to resolve the conflict between a sense of identity and its concomitant option, that of identity diffusion. The youth expresses himself socially by either being himself or not being himself, and by sharing this self with others. Ideologies, the perspectives they throw on life, and the settling influence they have on people become important options for the youth as a sense of trustworthiness is formed.

After identity's adolescent crisis, Erikson labels the crisis to be resolved as being "beyond identity." With a yet immature sense of identity the young adult now finds a time to fuse his identity with others. The conflicts are between intimacy—the capacity to commit oneself to partnerships, and isolation—to remain with oneself and alone.[72]

The ego strength developed in this stage is that of love which is "a mutuality of devotion forever subduing the antagonisms inherent in divided function."[73] Since this kind of love pervades individuals, it becomes the basis for ethical action. Because this crisis is significant in the forming of intimate ties in the ever-widening social context, others begin to play a significant part. Here identity is reflected in others and their relationships confirm or obscure identity itself.

The person in the young adult years finds himself attempting to resolve the crisis of intimacy vs. isolation, which manifests itself in trying to find himself in others and in himself. The traditional social patterns of cooperation and competition aid in the ascendance of this crisis with the hoped-for outcome of love.

The seventh stage is generativity versus stagnation. Generativity as a crisis simply means that man is so made up as to demand to be needed or else he will suffer the mental "deformation of self-absorption, in which he becomes his own infant and pet."[74] It is here that the psychosocial stage of generativity finds its source. Parenthood for Erikson is the first generative crisis, but it is broadened as a general form of being needed and knowing how to fill the needs. Generativity is "the concern in establishing and guiding the next generation."[75] Generativity includes the concepts of creativity and productivity, but is not to be solely associated with either of them. Without generativity, the person becomes self-absorbed or stagnated and is useless for himself or society. Stagnation is often expressed through a regression to a pseudo-intimacy which may be quite obsessive. Generativity has a peculiar relationship with the life cycle for it goes directly back to the first stage—that of establishing a sense of basic trust, or a belief in man himself.[76]

The social modalities for this stage are "to make be and to take care of."[77] These are expressed in the home, in the division of labor, and in a sense of shared householding. As to the institutions which reinforce generativity and safeguard it, Erikson claims that all institutions by their very nature codify the ethics which are related to generativity. For it is "generativity itself" which is a driving power in human organization.[78]

The virtue that emerges with generativity is care. Care is "the widening concern for what has been generated by love, necessity, or accident; it overcomes the ambivalence adhering to irreversible obligation."[79] As adult man needs to be needed, so for the benefit of his own ego and for that of his community itself, he requires the challenge that stems from what he has generated and from what now must be guarded, preserved, and even eventually transcended.[80]

It seems then that the person faces the ascendancy of this conflict in the middle years in attempts to resolve the crisis of generativity vs. stagnation, which manifests the modality of making be and taking care of. All social institutions by a kind of generative ethic develop the virtue of caring.

The final stage of development is validated by the crisis of ego integrity vs. despair or disgust. Integrity is not easily defined, and Erikson points to some attributes of this stage of mind to clarify it. It is first the accrued "assurance of its proclivity for order and meaning—an emotional integration faithful to the image bearers of the past and ready to take, and eventually to renounce, leadership in the present." Second, it is the acceptance of one's one and only life cycle and an acceptance of realizing that there are no substitutions at this point in the cycle. Third, it means then a new and different love of one's parents which is free from wanting them to be different or wishing them to be different. Fourth, it is a sense of oneness with men and women of the past which creates feelings of dignity and love. The social modality in this stage is like the "courage to be" of Tillich in the face of the paradox of being and not being. For it is to be, even though one has been, and to face not being itself. The wisdom that can be found in social institutions feeds this stage, and prepares the person to face death. The virtue which emerges in this stage is wisdom, which is for Erikson "the form of that detached yet active concern with life bounded by death. . . ."[81]

Since Erikson's input is so massive on identity formation, I believe there are criticisms that must be suggested regarding his research and theory. For example, one may raise questions as to whether or not the epigenetic principle can be validated at all. It is much easier to validate psychosexual theory than this, for in dealing with the psychosocial realm suggestions as to the relationship of culture and society can only be assumed but cannot definitely be proved or the actual empirical effects noted. Erikson must be complimented in using his scheme as a pattern and suggestion rather than the basis for empirical observation. For the ego is a construct; its being a reality is not the issue at all, and Erikson is justified in conceiving the identity formation in terms of ego development for the sake of illustration—as long as he is not found simply playing a word game with abstract functions.

Erikson is criticized for holding a presupposition of psychic determinism. Some events are determined, adding societal input; others are affected, but not all are. It is suggested that such things as creative thought and holding out during brainwashing are examples of this.[82] One major objection voiced here which parallels that of the study of conversion is that both Erikson and many researchers studying conversion phenomena rely on studying those individuals who deviate from the norm. Surely one learns much from studying the abnormal development of individuals, but how much more could be learned from examining those in peak health. Maslow criticizes this also and indicates that psychologists should seek to find the healthiest, maturest, and most actively productive persons to learn of normal development.[83]

We might criticize his cycle itself in its tendency to isolate individuals in an escalating approach to living, making others view people with a mind to analyzing which stage they are in. Erikson, however, suggests the cycle not be used as a scale, but rather as an indicator of development.

RELIGION AND IDENTITY

Older people often look at the identity struggle as just an intragenerational problem. Youth accuse age of unglueing the world. A world seems left which only reflects unstable patterns. Yet personal identity is formed within the context of unstable patterns, even crises, as we have seen in Erikson. What emerges is a stable pattern, a context out of which life begins to be ordered. An identity is beginning to be formed.

Identity has a close relationship with religion in general. Religion tells man who he is—a child of God; what he is—one in need of saving; where he belongs—in the family of God; how to belong to God—through commitment to God; how to relate to others—in loving, caring responses; and what man's future is—identity with God.

The biblical sense of a plan of salvation, wherein man is seen struggling back to God, helped by God, at home in God's care are recurring themes in Scripture. The account of the fall of man in Genesis emphasizes the need to return to the God who gives identity and fulfillment, and the eschatological theme of Ezekiel, Daniel, and Revelation suggests that restoration of man in God's image after his pilgrimage in a sinful world is really an identity function. The story of the early Christian church workers and their struggle to find out who they really were focused when they are finally called Christians. They followed Jesus. Being in Christ is an identity theme itself.

St. Peter in his attempt to walk on water sinks mercilessly until he looks to Jesus in trust to find a new direction. The symbolism is noteworthy. Jesus, for Christians, becomes the one who gives direction and purpose in life.

Identity themes in religion are not new or only located within the Christian tradition. In Hinduism this issue has always been basic. Hinduism sees the only real goal for man as his reuniting with Brahman in a close identification, that through yoga he might be reunited with his divine essence.[84]

Richard Fenn suggests that, "Religion inevitably grounds identity in unchanging symbols and so redresses imbalance between adaptation and stability, differentiation, and integration."[85]

Religion fails if its adherents cease to provide a meaningful system which transcends life itself and becomes the fabric of choices and values. One way to determine religion's success in the world is to observe the deep, ultimate values which it generates and creates. Likewise, personal experience with God must provide and generate and reflect real values if it is to have this stabilizing effect and sovereignty in the life which Christianity claims.

I remember hearing Paul Irwin claim that religion and the church fail if they do not encourage the disciples of critical thought to shape a vision of life that can provide intelligent dissent. Religion's main function is providing a vision of what might be in a world learning how to become.

Hans Mol would even suggest that one might look at a church's effect on attendance to see if it's meeting the identity needs of its membership or not.[86]

Religion, however, is a very general term and often just

means the thing your life revolves around. In this general kind of category, such things as football, hockey games, even stamp collecting can become religious issues. But in order for religion to really be "religious" there must be a sense of an "other" there, almost in the sense of Otto's concerns about the "holy." There is, however, another relationship which is significant, and that is the function of theology in the identity process.

Theology and thinking about God are close allies of the identity theory. The doctrine of God in most traditions includes allegiance to the god or "other", which we worship. The object of devotion transcends us while, at the same time, it is imminent within us. The doctrine of God in the Christian tradition invites us to consider the necessity of God revealing himself clearly in the history of the world in tangible ways.

G. Ernest Wright emphasizes this aspect in his profound book, *The God Who Acts*, when he suggests, "This (Christian) community exists and finds its true life in its responsibility and living relationships with God and its Lord."[87] Other allusions to the personal identity quality of religion are found in the Pauline image of the "body" of Christ with Jesus as the head, and the Johannine images of the vine with branches. There is an answer to the identity quest in response and commitment to God. Man and God become one, so to speak, in union together as man participates with God. He participates in an almost mystic way with the purposes of God, and therefore his life becomes ordered.

The Old Testament does not carry these New Testament themes; however, this personal identity found in relationship with God is a common Jewish theme. For example, the concept of "community" and "corporate personality" reflect this. In the Old Testament God is seen as the

One who can recreate the community of the saints. He does it through a renewed covenant, one of peace and not war and dissension. The reason man could be at peace was that he was in relationship with God. The God of Israel was always conceived as a person, and "there was no surer way of deepening our own personality than fellowship with the Greater One."[88] It was characteristic that the national unification of Israel would be generated and even maintained by its identity with God. The knowledge of being a part of prophetic consciousness kept Israel's identity and does, even today, in contemporary Jewish communities.

In the world there is always a need for men who will be strong to inner motives, who will be true to the sense of right and truth which they sense revealed, and with this intense commitment to their purpose in life comes the sense of identification with the One who gives them direction. Through obedience to "true calling" one participates in the identity of God. When one disobeys (sins) in the biblical sense, he separates himself from the one true person who models life, and in a sense loses his real identity. Or, as Paul Tillich claims, "Sin is primarily and basically the power of turning away from God. For this reason, no moral remedy is possible. Only one remedy is adequate—a return to God."[89]

God becomes the "eternal now," *nunc aeternum,* who meets man where he is, and who he is, and does not ask for a kind of moral goodness to prove he is deserving. Rather, God encounters man and gives freely his peaceful presence and purpose in man's estrangement. Resting in God through faithful response brings God's identity to man's empty life, and man knows he is kept by God.

The new birth concept in Scripture provides a New Testament allusion to this process of identification, only this time with Jesus. Nicodemus is pictured in John 3 waiting to engage Jesus with theological possibilities.

"Surely you are a teacher. How else could you do what you do?"

"Verily, I say unto you, unless a man is born from above, he will never see God's kingdom."

"How can that be?" came the response.

The discussion went further. Nicodemus approaches the question by Jesus as with any analytical thinker and tries to identify rebirth in a physical sense. Jesus shows him his belief problem and suggests that through water and spirit one is reborn and participates in heavenly things. If, in the water allusion, baptism is referred to, we have a beautiful symbol of personal identity here. Death, burial and resurrection become the New Testament means of participation with Jesus, and by extension, with God himself. Jesus adds to this belief in Christ as the final step of securing salvation and existence and meaning with his concluding speech in John 3:16, "For God so loved the world that he gave his only begotten Son that whosoever believes in him shall not perish but have everlasting life."

Within the definitions of personal identity we have obvious correlations with religion's function. Personal identity as "that stable niche" reflects the personhood of man in relation with the stable, knowing God. Since personal identity seems anchored in a transcendent order symbolized by religion and God-consciousness, personal identity finds a close friend in identity itself. As others look at the coherence within one's sense of personal identity reflected by values and purposes, choices and important symbols, religion and God-knowledge generate personal identity. Reflecting opinions and masking and/or mirroring one's role bring the personhood of Christians in relationship to a personal God to the front. With the expectations religion

offers and within the understandings of theological implications about God, man sees where he fits and what is of
real value in life. He can grow and respond in a comfortable way. He understands how he fits because his relationship is in God, so to speak. Even within the crisis of growth
and life situations the cycle of personal and ego identity
relate to religion. Opportunities to grow, or in Sherrillian
terms, "shrink back," provide opportunities to become
stable and self-wise in knowing who we are in relationship
to God. The question still remains, however: What is the
experience like? How is it experienced? Erik Erikson again
seems to be an eloquent spokesman for our understanding
of this experience.

NOTES

1. Ephesians 1:3-6, *New English Bible.*
2. David J. De LeVita, *The Concept of Identity* (Paris: Mouton &
Co., 1965), p. 3.
3. A. M. Becker, "Kindheit, Gesellschaft and Inclantität,"
Psyche, XI, 1956, p. 536 or see De LeVita's introduction to identity formation in his book listed above.
4. Personal letter from Erik Erikson, Stockbridge, Mas-
sachusetts, October 26, 1972.
5. Anselm L. Strauss, *Mirrors & Masks: The Search for Identity*
(Glencoe, Ill.: Free Press, 1959), p. 9.
6. De LeVita, *Concept of Identity,* p. 13.
7. Ibid., p. 14.
8. Ibid., pp. 32-40.
9. Erik Erikson, "Identity and the Life Cycle," *Psychological
Issues,* I, No. 1 (New York: International Universities Press, Inc.,
1959), pp. 101-102.
10. Ibid.
11. Mary Howard Dignam, "Ego Identity of the Modern Re-

ligious Woman," *Journal of Religion & Health,* VI, No. 2 (April, 1967), p. 107.

12. Erik H. Erikson, *Identity: Youth and Crises* (New York: W. W. Norton and Co., Inc., 1968), pp. 19–20.

13. Ibid., p. 22.

14. Ibid.

15. Erikson, "Identity and the Life Cycle," p. 102.

16. De LeVita, *Concept of Identity,* p. 105.

17. Ibid., p. 108.

18. Hans J. Mol, *Identity and the Sacred* (New York: The Free Press, 1976), p. 59.

19. See Thomas Luckmann, *The Invisible Religion* (New York: The Macmillan Co., 1967), pp. 77–106.

20. Mol, *Identity and the Sacred,* p. 65.

21. Ibid.

22. Ibid., pp. 59–60.

23. Ibid.

24. Ibid., pp. 143, 144.

25. George J. McCall and J. L. Simmons, *Identities and Interactions* (New York: The Free Press, 1966), p. 64.

26. Mol, *Identity and the Sacred,* pp. 143, 144.

27. Allen Wheelis, *The Quest for Identity* (New York: W. W. Norton & Co., 1958), p. 18.

28. Ibid., p. 19.

29. Ibid., p. 200.

30. Ibid., p. 174.

31. Allen Wheelis, "Psychoanalysis and Identity," *Psychoanalysis and the Psychoanalytic Review,* 46, 1959, p. 71.

32. Wheelis, *Quest for Identity,* pp. 21, 22.

33. Mol, *Identity and the Sacred,* p. 58.

34. See Lynn Mallery, "Changing Roles of Laity and Ministry," paper presented at the West Coast Religion Teachers' Conference, Walla Walla, Washington, April 1978.

35. Anselm Strauss quoted in De LeVita, *Concept of Identity,* p. 96.

36. Strauss, *Mirrors and Masks: The Search for Identity,* p. 66.

37. Ibid., pp. 90, 91.

38. Erikson, "Identity and the Life Cycle," p. 23ff, and *Identity: Youth and Crises,* p. 174ff.

39. Erikson, *Identity: Youth and Crises,* p. 50.

40. Dignam, "Ego Identity of the Modern Religious Woman," p. 106.

41. Erik Erikson, "Memorandum on Identity and Negro Youth," *The Journal of Social Issues*, XX, No. 4 (1964), p. 31.

42. The terms "negative identity" and "identity diffusion" or confusion will be defined later; until then, it is significant only to understand them as those drives which would inhibit, deter, or misshape the finding of a healthy sense of identity, as far as the person is concerned.

43. Erikson, *Identity: Youth and Crises*, p. 23.

44. See Erik Erikson, *Young Man Luther* (New York: W. W. Norton and Co., Inc., 1958), pp. 14–25.

45. Erikson, *Identity: Youth and Crises*, p. 24.

46. Dignam, "Ego Identity of the Modern Religious Woman," p. 109.

47. Ibid., p. 110.

48. Erikson, "Identity and the Life Cycle," p. 52.

49. Erik Erikson, *Insight and Responsibility* (New York: W. W. Norton and Co., Inc., 1964), pp. 132–133.

50. Ibid., p. 114.

51. Erikson, *Identity: Youth and Crises*, pp. 93, 95.

52. Erikson, *Young Man Luther*, p. 20.

53. Erikson, "Identity and the Life Cycle," p. 53.

54. Richard I. Evans, *Dialogue with Erik Erikson* (New York: E. P. Dutton and Co., 1969), p. 15.

55. Mistrust is used in the sense of a readiness for danger and an anticipation of discomfort and must be learned in the context of the culture to which we belong.

56. Erikson, *Insight and Responsibility*, p. 118.

57. H. R. Bagwell, "Abrupt Religious Conversion Experience," *Journal of Religion and Health*, VIII (April, 1969), p. 53, quoting Erik Erikson, "Wholeness and Totality: A Psychiatric Contribution," *Totalitarianism*, ed. by Carl Friedrich (Proceedings of a conference held at the American Academy of Arts and Sciences, March, 1953; (Cambridge, Mass.: Harvard University Press, 1954), p. 164.

58. Evans, *Dialogue with Erik Erikson*, p. 18.

59. Ibid., p. 20.

60. Erikson, "Identity and the Life Cycle," p. 70.

61. Erikson, *Insight and Responsibility*, p. 119.

62. Ibid., p. 120.
63. Erikson, *Identity: Youth and Crises,* p. 114.
64. Erikson, *Insight and Responsibility,* p. 122.
65. Erikson, *Identity: Youth and Crises,* p. 124.
66. Ibid., p. 127.
67. Erikson, *Insight and Responsibility,* p. 124.
68. Erikson, *Young Man Luther,* pp. 12-39.
69. Erikson, *Identity: Youth and Crises,* p. 134.
70. Erikson, "Identity and the Life Cycle," pp. 91-93.
71. Erikson, *Insight and Responsibility,* p. 125.
72. Erikson, *Identity: Youth and Crises,* p. 125.
73. Erikson, *Insight and Responsibility,* p. 129.
74. Ibid., p. 130.
75. Erik Erikson, *Childhood and Society* (New York: W. W. Norton and Co., Inc., 1963), p. 267.
76. Erikson, "Identity and the Life Cycle," p. 97.
77. Ibid., p. 166.
78. Erikson, *Identity: Youth and Crises,* p. 139.
79. Erikson, *Insight and Responsibility,* p. 131.
80. Ibid.
81. Erikson, *Identity: Youth and Crises,* p. 140.
82. Erikson, *Childhood and Society,* p. 74.
83. Abraham Maslow, *Toward a Psychology of Being* (Princeton: D. Van Nostrand Co., Inc., 1962), pp. 5-35.
84. F. H. Ross, *The Meaning of Life in Hinduism and Buddhism* (London: Routledge and Kegan Paul, 1953), p. ix.
85. Richard Fenn, *Journal for the Scientific Study of Religion,* XVII, No. 1 (March, 1978), pp. 67-68.
86. Mol, *Identity and the Sacred,* p. 82.
87. G. Ernest Wright, *The God Who Acts* (London: SCM Press, Ltd., 1964), p. 98.
88. H. Wheeler Robinson, *Corporate Personality in Ancient Israel* (Penn: Fortress Press, 1964), pp. 28-29.
89. Paul Tillich, *A History of Christian Thought* (New York: Harper & Row, 1968), p. 127.

CHAPTER V

IDENTITY: The Context of Faith

"I was brought up Church of England, you know, and baptized, and then at Marlborough, I suddenly decided I was an atheist and refused to be confirmed. I used to think that religion was hymn singing and feeling good and not being immoral and always having a high moral tone and really rather priggish. Until... I remember one summer bicycling about in Cornwall and coming to a church, St. Irvin, in North Cornwall and meeting the vicar there who was a nice eccentric, and he said, I suppose you think religion is hymn singing in the chapel at Marlborough. And I said—Yes. And he said: Well—read this... Arthur Machens' *Secret Glory,* which suddenly showed me there were the Sacraments, and then I became very interested in ritual, and I was first, I suppose, brought to belief by my eyes and ears and nose.... I do see that behind all the ritual and everything like that, the one fundamental thing is that Christ was God. And it's very hard to believe—it's a very hard thing to swallow. But if you believe it, it gives some point to everything and really I don't think life would be worth living if it weren't true." John Betjeman's *Diary.*

Coming to God and becoming one of his children in fact rather than in theological theory brings home directly into the life the things about God which are valuable. Like John Betjeman's experience, coming to God through conversional return "gives some point to everything." Identity, like the result of the religious conversion process, brings into life not a quantity, but rather a quality that pervades the life of an individual. Personal identity, and in a deeper sense and at a more conscious level, ego identity, are influenced by factors not entirely unlike those of the religious conversion experience. Identity is influenced by factors and molded in the life spaces and cultural context of an individual. More specifically now we look to the crisis decision experience of identity and the formation of identity as it is experienced, contrasted with the parallels that can be drawn from religious conversion experience.

Since religious conversion's product is new beliefs and values, and identity often results in religious values, the close relationship is evident. Religion provides for youth and adults a theology (ideology) and a resource for peace among men.[1] Erik Erikson even hopes religion would provide a means for bringing out the humanity of man and would provide a world image "sustaining hope" for youth and for the weak.[2]

Religion's role, as suggested in the last chapter, is that of guarantor for the parents' faith, so that the youth may reflect from their parents what is meaningful and right. Since personal identity first deals with a sense of basic trust, it is this trusting quality in the parents' values which, through interaction with the youth or growing child, provides the identity tags for religious growth, and through these stable identity tags promotes return to God for the returning child of God. The parental gift of providing the kind of faith which so permeates the parents' personalities that it reinforces the child's sense of basic confidence in the world's trustworthiness becomes a first step in the religious conversion process. In order for someone to return, one must begin that return, and in parenting, the stages of personal identity begin.

In this change process, however, desire to be recognized

becomes very important. Personal identity demands knowing who one really is. So it is with religious conversion experience. Being known by God is just as important. The first step in both processes is to become recognized. Erik Erikson states it most beautifully:

> In the Judeo-Christian tradition, no prayer indicates this more clearly than "The Lord make his face to shine upon you and be gracious unto you. The Lord lift up his countenance upon you and give you peace;" and no prayerful attitude is better than the uplifted face, hopeful of being recognized. The Lord's countenance is apt to loom too sternly, and his Son's on the cross to show the enigmatic quality of total abandonment in sacrifice. . . . [3]

One major role of religious conversion and religion is to promote basic trust, which is simply the childlike trust developed in the first stages of life. Coming face to face with God and personal religious conversion allows the opposite stance to be taken as well—mistrust, doubt, and shame, the counterparts to true trust and faith. As new ideologies are formulated, new theologies begun, new beliefs practiced and pondered, the grappling with doubt and mistrust merge into faith and promise. It was through this grappling that Martin Luther believed finally who he was, and what it was he was to believe. Religious conversion's confrontation of the person with ideologies and theological presuppositions fulfills this need as well. Erik Erikson again posits that in some periods of the history of the world and in "some phases of his life cycle, man needs (until we invent something better) a new ideological orientation as surely and as sorely as he must have air and food."[4]

There is, in religious conversion, a feeling tone of conviction essential for personal identity, the same conviction and feeling tone that exists in the identity-forming crisis. This conviction gives Christians a feeling of community and a sense of the eternal—something to die for, as it were. This sense of reality and this strength of conviction aid in solidifying personal identity. Religious conversional return aids in personal identity formation through this function.

If religious institutions only stress the feelings of conviction as important, there is, then, a danger that religious institutions will become so engrossed in rejuvenation by the emotional reinvestment of the generations that they will lose their reason for existence. When religion no longer provides hope and meaningful relationships within the community of faith, it will end up lost in delusion, addiction, and lost ethics. Religion at this point, and the process of returning to God typified by religious conversion experience, will just be fostering illusions, empty promises, and probably fantasy.[5]

For many today, a personal religious experience not related to identification with a diety has taken over where religion has stopped. The secular ideologies present themselves as pillars upon which to reflect the past and around which to organize individual faith. Paralleling religion, these secular ideologies tend to counteract and promote a sense of alienation and their own positive ritual and "affirmative dogma." They "do not hesitate to combine magic with technique by amplifying the sound of one voice speaking out of the night, and by magnifying and multiplying one face in the spotlights of mass gatherings."[6]

Religion's major role, then, is in providing a framework of ideology, as well as giving one an experiential knowledge of deity out of which feelings and emotions grow.

Two specific studies are helpful in seeing the relationship of personal identity with religious conversion experience. Erik Erikson's *Young Man Luther* and *Gandhi's Truth* treat both religious conversion and personal ego identity. These two books deal with the development of identity through the life cycle of two historically great men. Insights as to how their identity and culture become internalized to produce historic personages rather than just people in history are given. Erikson for one does not try to define the experience of conversion; neither does he try to delineate its source other than to suggest the mental function operant in the change. He simply deals with the experience as a real happening and a means for change in the lives of people. In his understanding of Paul's conversion, for example, he contrasts it with that of Luther. He suggests that Paul's was a kind of heroic conversion. Paul was neither too young or provincial, was of cosmopolitan origin, in public life, and not a Christian. He was a deputy prosecutor for the high priest's office, actively engaged, "engaged fully: breathing out threatenings and slaughter," in the mission of prosecuting the Damascan Christians. His conversion on the road was not only immediately certified as being "of apostolic dimension by God's independent message to Ananias; it also immediately became equivalent to a political act, for Paul, the prosecutor, took sides with the defendants whom he committed to bring to justice."[7] In addition to stressing the definitive kind of change conversion is, Erikson contrasts Luther with Paul.

> There is only one similarity between Luther's experience and Paul's which can be formulated only by somewhat stretching a point. The two men, at the time of their conversions, were both engaged in the law, one as an advanced functionary responsible to the high priest, the other as a student owing obedience to the father. Both, through their conversion, received the message that there is a higher obedience than the law, in either of these connotations, and that this obedience brooks no delay.[8]

Both were shaken by an attack that went to the core of their experience, affecting both body and psyche. The religious conversions of these two men show the same intensity. Both were "thrown to the ground" in more or less psychological states. Some attribute the symptoms to epilepsy for Paul. But they both testify to a dramatic turnaround conversion provided. In one case, however, Paul had been prepared for some kind of a change of mind, in the "kicking against the pricks" statement, for example, which the New Testament indicates. But for Luther, there was a more intrapsychic conversion. Erikson states Luther never claimed for himself that he had heard or seen anything supernatural. Luther only claimed that "something in him made him pronounce a vow before the rest of him knew what he was saying."[9] Others' confirmation of his changed life was an important factor validating the change for young Martin, and "Martin can claim for his conversion only ordinary psychological attributes, except for his professed conviction that it was God who had directed an otherwise ordinary thunderstorm straight toward him."[10]

Erikson and others would attribute many of the causes of conversion to psychological causes, but in so doing do not belittle the sincerity of Luther and the meaning for the life that these decisions had nor the decisiveness of the experience.

The change in Luther's life committed him to being monos, a "professional monk among many."[11] In fact, the real issue at this time was whether Martin should go home to face his father after his conviction; thus the conversion to become a monk was to provide him a moratorium in which to find himself, as well as a negative identity as a solution to the problem of diffusion. The feelings Erikson describes as existing in identity formation have already been illustrated; these he sees illustrated in the preconversion state of young Luther.

The situation in the train station and the following events in advocating a nonviolent position constitute the conversion for Gandhi. A factor referred to as an element of conversion is *sincerity;* both Luther and Gandhi were sincere. The conversion experience is unique for its total psychosocial involvement which, according to Erikson, is significant even if you attribute it to inspiration or to temporarily abnormal behavior. The uniqueness of these experiences is that they gave a decisive inner push to a youth in search of an identity within a given cultural situation and provided the ideological commitment which is so necessary for fidelity and identity to be developed and experienced.

The question for those interested in identity is not whether religious conversion is valid in terms of theological truth, but whether it is a part of identity. We can say affirmatively that this is so. The religious conversion experience provides a turning point in the life of the young person and answers the questions raised when the youth faces the problem of just what he is going to give his life to or for. Through religious conversion's experience, an all-embracing goal is obtained and focused, around which the experiences of life will be grounded and interpreted.

The outcome of identity experience does not have to be a religious one, but in the cases of Gandhi and Luther it was. Religious conversion leads to a formulated faith either implicitly given or endowed to the youth through adults.[12] For the Christian, religious conversion implies a God direction, and it is here that the biblical scholar parts with the psychologist.

Although Erikson is quick to judge many conversions and God-oriented decisions as being a part of pathology, he also feels that many decisions for religious values are a means of finding identity by first perceiving God face to face as through a glass darkly, then emerging to the full light of his presence.[13] This he does not criticize.

IDENTITY EXPERIENCE

The identity crisis is simply a normative process and is the psychosocial aspect of adolescing. The time-space when identity decisions are the most experienced is thought of as the period from adolescence to the early twenties. This stage cannot be passed without identity experiences specifically occurring which will determine the youth's later life. The experience is considered *normal* and even *necessary* for the youth to determine his role. It is a normal crisis characterized by more reversibility or transversibility than would be found in more psychotic crises which are characterized by a self-perpetuating tendency, by an increasing amount of energy for ego defensive purposes, and by feelings of intense psychosocial isolation.

Some have called the major identity forming experience a "crisis" which occurs in that period of the life cycle when the young person senses a need to find out for himself the central core experiences of his being, some central perspective and direction, some "working unity out of the effective remnants of his childhood and the hopes of his anticipated adulthood."[14] The youth is detecting through the crisis some meaningful resemblance between what he believes himself to be and what he is aware others judge him to be.

Gordon Allport suggests that a crisis is a situation of emotional and mental stress which requires some significant alterations of outlook within a short period of time.

Some of these alterations of outlook frequently involve some kind of change in the very structure of the personality. The results may be progressive or regressive in the life as others perceive it, yet in crisis a person "cannot stand still; that is to say, he cannot redact his present traumatic experience into familiar and routine categories or imply a simple habitual mode of adjustment."[15] The *movement* in crisis is toward resolving it. The youth must either find himself separated further from his childhood moving toward adulthood, or find himself moving backward to earlier levels of adjustment which may be experienced in disorganization, dropping out, or leaving the field of perspective. These backward movements result in perceived hostilities and defenses. The youth may become a thorn in the flesh of the teacher, parent, dean, or pastor, yet the crisis may not become stabilized until after months of disorganization.

A person is never "an adult adult, was a childlike child, nor became an adolescent adolescent without what Piaget calls conflict—a matter to which I would give a more normative and developmental status by calling it crisis."[16] The crisis in identity is not a catastrophe; rather, it should be used in a medical sense where it connotes a crucial period in which a decisive action of movement is implied or is even perhaps unavoidable. These crises occur in man's total development sometimes more noisily when there are new needs which meet internal or perceived prohibitions, and they occur more quietly when the needs are simply a yearning to match new opportunities. Youth's disruption of the life cycle with its conflictual scheme tends to emphasize the crisis nature better than simply listing the crisis. He presents a dynamic picture of the movement within the developing ego of the youth, and in this way, during identity's crucial period, the adolescent through crisis must find identity or be led to a possible sense of role confusion. Conversion—the return to the family of God—becomes a vital identity-forming experience. The identity experience itself becomes the *sense of contending forces striving for resolution.*

The source for identity has an unusually simple explanation for Erikson. "Before Darwin the answer was clear: because God created Adam in his own image, as a counterplayer of his identity, and thus, bequeathed to all man the glory and the despair of individuation and faith. I admit to not having come up with any better explanation."[17]

These crisis moments of decision when identity is realized or at least identity formation begins occur for some rapidly when various choices and paths are easily seen and decided upon permanently. At the same time a gradual sense of crisis in identity can be seen. These decisions reflect those of earlier times and the successful working through of the major epigenetic crisis. Yet the experience itself is defined as being a sense of divergency and discomfort with decisions resolving the crisis and therefore emphasizing the point of resolution and direction change.[18]

Another aspect of the identity experience itself is an intense *need for devotion.* This is an aspect of the identity crisis which is a drive to establish a meaningful world view, one that can be believed in, to which youth can commit himself, in which he seeks satisfaction.

In their late teens and early twenties, even when there is no explicit ideological commitment or even interest, young people offer devotion to individual leaders and to teams, to strenuous activities, and to difficult techniques; at the same time they show a sharp and intolerant readiness to discard and disavow people (including, at times, themselves). This repudiation is often snobbish, fitful, perverted, or simply thoughtless.[19]

It is during this time that ideologies play a role in identity and provide the content for devotion in the experience. Ideologies offer to the members of this age group simple but determined answers to exactly those vague inner states and those urgent questions that come through the identity experience. Ideologies serve to "channel youth's forceful earnestness and sincere asceticism, as well as its search for excitement and its eager indignation, toward that social frontier where the struggle between conservatism and radicalism is most alive."[20] You will remember conversion's relationship to ideology. One does not return unless he returns *to* something. The individuals healed by Jesus were invited to go on "the way"—with the obvious implications of discipleship and understanding of "the way."

When man asks existential questions about being—and man seems to ask them more intensely during this period of life than others—it is easy to see the role that an intense belief system has for identity experience. In an attempt to solve his being, ideologies provide answers and resolutions to the quest for meaning in life and provide a stabilizing resolution to the experience expressed in crisis of identity.

Another expression of the experience of personal and ego identity is the *feeling tones of the experience* itself. It seems that the crisis is expressed in similar terms as is the religious conversion crisis. There is a pre-state demonstrated by anxiety and conflict. The following quotation, used before in part, will demonstrate the feelings some see surrounding identity.

I have called the major crisis of adolescence the *identity* crisis; it occurs in that period of the life cycle when each youth must forge for himself some central perspective and direction, some working unity, out of the effective remnants of his childhood and the hope of his anticipated adulthood. . . . He must detect some meaningful resemblance between what he has come to see in himself, and what his sharpened awareness tells him others judge and expect him to be. . . . In some young people, in some classes, at some periods in history, this crisis will be minimal; in other people, classes and periods, the crisis will be clearly marked off as a critical period, a kind of "second birth," apt to be aggravated either by widespread neuroticism or by pervasive ideological unrest. Some young individuals will succumb to this crisis in all manner of neurotic, psychotic, or delinquent behavior; others will resolve it through participation in ideological movements, passionately concerned with religion or politics, nature, or art. . . .[21]

Noted here is the graphic portrayal of *conflict at the core of being,* a conflict with anxiety at its base seeking solution to alternative views about self and life. Its intensity is demonstrated and suggested to have neurotic or healthy results. Erikson illustrated a preidentity state in his analysis of Martin Luther's major crisis in life. He describes Luther's general mood before he became a monk as one of *tristitia* (or excessive sadness). The feelings came to Luther before the thunderstorm, when he had been slowly slipping into a melancholy paralysis making it hard for the young Luther to continue his schooling and marry, as his father had urged him to do. During the thunderstorm, he felt intense anxiety, feeling hemmed in and choked up. Erikson suggests that Luther's use of *circumvallatus,* meaning in Latin "all walled in" is significant to describe the intensity of the emotions before the identity-forming experience.[22] This constriction of one's whole life space in which one sees no particular way out except through the giving up of a previous life style and all earthly future for the sake of total devotion to a new form of living depicts an extreme identity struggle for Luther and illustrates the kind of feeling tones associated with the preidentity experience.

Gordon Allport adds to Erikson's insight a list of statements that describe feelings existing before resolution of a conflict in young adults. These typical statements of crisis feelings illustrate a sense of lostness and despair-seeking-solution.

1. I feel I have been dragged into something against my will.
2. I feel like a rat in a maze.
3. I was to be a law unto myself, but cannot. It seems suddenly that the decisions I make must be valid for the rest of my life.
4. The lives of the past and the life of the future seems suddenly to be at cross purposes.[23]

Even though apathy may be experienced while going through these crises, it is only a mask for anxiety deep within.

The causes of identity conflict are many—the physiological revolution of genital maturation including feelings of uncertainty about the adult roles, and a search for some sense of continuity and sameness inside the person. Many causes find their source in the events outside the person. Illustrating this, Erikson cites a crisis in Gandhi's life which precipitated identity formation and caused anxiety about himself. The crisis was in the middle age of this great man and is used as an example of a significant time when Gandhi solved his identity crisis. The experience happened in the railroad station of Maritzburg, South Africa, when the lawyer made a trip and was ejected from the train because he insisted in traveling first class even though he was recongized as a "coolie" or "colored." At this point, brought on by external circumstances, he abandoned his shy self and, literally at once, radically commited himself to his political and religious destiny as a leader. Even though Gandhi was nearly fifty years old at the time, the individuals he gathered around him were at their identity peak and found in him fulfillment of their ideological needs, and his views became a part of their identity structure.[24]

Another outside influence effective in causing identity conflict is the *relationship of culture*. Sociologists cite cases of social transportation and cultural deprivation through transmigration which caused identity conflict and posed anxiety-filled situations which aided in individuals finding their place in life. They suggest that there is a danger in any period of large scale uprooting that this exterior crisis will upset the natural ascendancy of inner concerns and pose a traumatic conflict needing resolution. When man loses his roots, roots that must be firmly founded in the life cycle, roots that "are nourished in the sequence of generations, he loses his taproots in disrupted developmental time, not in abandoned localities."[25] This transmigration is a collective crisis and results in the production of new and very intense world images. Oftentimes, these images demand sudden assimilation of the new, and wholeness and initiative are shattered. Wholeness and initiative are attributes of identity and are therefore damaged in the moving in a very deep way. This sense of "rootlessness" has a deep effect and causes identity anxiety to be pronounced, while a knowledge of belonging permeates the religious conversion state by contrast.

There are additional *internal sources* for identity crisis and the feeling tones that correspond to the experience as well, and they are reminiscent of religious conversion crises. Luther again is a good example. Some three or more distinct and fragmentary experiences for Luther which gave impetus for his identity can be cited. Some receive these qualities in one explosive event, while Luther may have had many. They are physical paroxysms, a degree of unconsciousness, an automatic verbal utterance, a command to change the overall direction of effort and aspiration, a spiritual revelation, and a flash of enlightenment which was decisive and pervasive like a rebirth. The thunderstorm had given him a "change in the overall direction of his life, a change toward the anonymous, the silent, and the obedient. In fits such as the one in the choir, he experienced the epileptoid paroxysm of ego-loss, the rage of denial of the identity which was to be discarded. And later in the experience in the tower, which . . . he perceived as the light of a new spiritual formula."[26] Here significant inner struggles are delineated. It is significant to note the experience developing even if we would deny the ego involvement. The development is from disunity and lack of identity, through events and inner struggles which provide impetus for unity and commitment, and finally the surety of a new formula for inner peace. The parallels with religious conversion experience are obvious.

Another internal cause for the crisis is the existential fear or dread which causes man to quest within and without his environment for promises of identity. The ego drive of wishing to be known along with such crises that stem from intellectual challenges are factors in conflict as well.

In summary, then, the experience of personal identity crisis finds in it the feeling tones of anxiety, depression, fragmentation, and concern for internal unity in the face of crises brought on through inner ego needs, outer cultural circumstances, and age-specific task fulfillment.

Regarding the identity experience itself, then, there is often in the pre-stages of the experience a morbid, often curious preoccupation with the conflicts that arise, stemming from early identifications and the successful working through of these identifications. Identity experience has a moment of decision, or more accurately stated, resolution, where through outer, inner, cultural, psychical, or even negatively worked-through identifications, a kind of giving up is experienced. This giving up is expressed in the finding of identity and the realization of one's place in the cosmos, or in a smaller sphere, finding meaning in one's decisions and position in life. Adolescence seems to be the stage wherein the ascendancy of this kind of crisis becomes prominent, and the resolution of the crisis tends toward faith which is being true to oneself and others, an ego result most desired for a healthy adult.

MORATORIUM

The setting for identity and its ensuing crisis is postulated as a kind of moratorium or time of reflection. The completion of ego identity takes place during this period, and it is a time permitted by society for a youth to experiment about his identity and major decisions in life. Since societies know that youth change rapidly even in their most intense devotions, they therefore should actually seek to give them a moratorium, or a span of time after they have ceased being children but before their deeds and works count toward a future identity. Erikson uses Luther an an example again of one going through such a moratorium. In Luther's time for that society, the monastery was, for some, one possible psychosocial moratorium. It was

> one possible way of postponing the decision as to what one is and what one is going to be. It may seem strange that as definite and, in fact, as eternal, a commitment as is expressed in the monastic vow could be considered a moratorium, a

means of marking time. Yet in Luther's era, to be an ex-monk was not impossible; nor was there necessarily a stigma attached to leaving a monastic order, provided only that one left in a quiet and prescribed way—as for example, Erasmus did, who was nevertheless offered a cardinalate in his old age. . . . I do not mean to suggest that those who choose the monastery any more than those who choose other forms of moratoria in different historical coordinates (as Freud did, in committing himself to laboratory physiology, or St. Augustine to Manichaeism) know that they are marking time before they come to their crossroad, which they often do in the late twenties, belated just because they gave their all to the temporary subject of devotion. The crisis in such a young man's life may be reached exactly when he half-realizes that he is fatally overcommitted to what he is not.[27]

This moratorium seems to be built into human development itself.[28] And like all the moratoria in man's developmental schedules, the delay of adulthood can be lengthened and intensified to a forceful and to a fateful degree by the culture, according to Erikson, at least. It is in this period that the youth finds time to experiment with the various ideologies and to quest for a ready niche in society. As the youth sees himself more clearly toward the close of this moratorium, he is able to bridge the span between infantile and childlike actions and meanings and become an adult. Identity discovered through this experience aids his self-conception and his society's recognition of him.[29] Society also plays a role in this intermixture of moratorium and culture. It has a responsibility to recognize more than just achievement in a person; it must validate his relationship to the whole of society. This kind of recognition aids the ego in the tasks of adolescing. Recognition maintains the ego defenses against the newly-vitalized impulses and consolidates the most "conflict-free" achievements in preparation for a job and resynthesizes the previous childhood identifications in life with the demands of society.[30]

The adult role in this moratorium is that of guide and advisor who corrects or confirms the youth. At all times, however, the youth must feel that he is the one making the choice. These attitudes youth find in adults validate adult guarantor roles as well as affirm in the youth some sort of consistency as he emerges from his necessary inner confusion.

Identity theory, you will remember, suggests the great importance of role experimentation in the formulation of a sense of identity. In addition to feelings of certainty and identity knowledge, role taking is a very important factor. Orrin Klapp suggests, "The student of identity must necessarily be deeply interested in interaction, for it is in and because of face-to-face interaction that so much appraisal—of self and others—occurs."[31] Role experimentation is simply the experimentation, so natural in adolescence, when various roles are tried on to see which fits. This quest for a role congruent with the emerging identity of the young person is a positive factor in identity formation.

The larger the field of choice in this role experimentation, the more possibilities for personal identity seem to emerge, and conversely so as well. If no choices exist for oneself, a negative identity, or so it would be called, would be manifest. The experimentation which engages youth is neither logical nor systematic. Youth find joy in rather abrupt and challenging roles which are not typical. Religion's role here is one of channeling the roles and experimentation through ritual, initiations, and confirmations. One problem for the adolescent is the fact that if the youth picks a particular role, he runs the risk of commitment to that role. These premature commitments do not prove to be as permanent as those which are developed after a long struggle with various possibilities.

If we use the life-cycle model in the formation of a healthy identity, the opposite function of identity might occur, and that is called negative identity, which simply means a youth may take on the identity of everything he has been told he should *not* become. It is an interesting phenomenon when a youth becomes something that he has been told or shown that he should not be. When youth are not allowed to experiment with various roles, they often adopt a negative one and assume its identity. Negative identity is not only a component of an unhealthy identity, but is also a *solution* to identity diffusion, at least for Erikson. When an individual finds himself confused or faced with the crisis of not knowing himself and how he fits, and the sameness and congruity that comes from identity is not present, a confusion or diffusion may be the result. It is here that a youth who has no identity seeks one, even in negative terms, and thus becomes something for awhile, even if he may not remain with this identity. Many a sick or desperate late adolescent, faced with continuing conflict, would just as soon be nobody, somebody totally bad, even dead by their choice, than be not quite somebody.[32]

The roots of this conflict, even though occurring in the stage of adolescence, have their beginnings in the third stage of the life cycle in the time of initiative versus guilt, for Erikson. Negative identity seems to be the result of the failure of a developing initiative and the dominance of guilt in this stage of the cycle. As individuals experience identity, sometimes the opposite effect seems to occur. Some theorists, such as Erikson, have suggested the term identity diffusion as the term used to describe the feeling tone for this crisis of adolescence. It is the splitting of the self, or the loss of the central core of one's being, the real loss of a sense of identity that is identity diffusion. Other theorists would simply explain this as identity confusion. Confusion about one's identity is not an orderly thing. In this process there is a loss of center. Factors that contribute to this identity kind of confusion, then, seem to be the same as those which function in identity for some. The key role is played by the acts of mutuality occurring in the developing ego growth. For example, there should be some type of mutual recognition between the youth and his peers in order for him to find his identity, as we have mentioned earlier in our discussion of identity theory. The role of adult guarantor is very important, not only for the ideological feedback and exemplary role that this person may fill, but for his own identity to be personally established. The youth must see himself in relationship to mature people who treat him with mutual respect and recognition. This gives his own sense of personal worth validation, as well as watching his own personhood in the interaction of life itself.

Jere Yates suggests some factors that should exist for a mutual recognition to occur: "1) a youth must be free enough from past problems to choose the important person or group; 2) there must be a person or group who is interested in the kind of youth that he actually is; and 3) cultural conditions must allow the two to meet."[33] Yates also suggests that when this mutual relationship does not exist, then confusion will set in. If a society finds its youth being just what the representatives of that society tell him he is, he has no real personal identity, and this sometimes will lead to great confusion and diffusion.[34] This role of others and the pressures they exert for change within the individual is significant for conversion as well, for the factors seem to be correlated in this area. More will be said about that later.

Most writers spend a great deal of time using adolescence as a major context of identity. The previous elements of identity, the ensuing identity crisis of diffusion, the adoption of a negative identity, and the development of the results of identity formation itself, both positively and negatively formed, show the centrality of adolescence for the time of formation. This context is a time of faith development for youth.

IDENTITY AND ADOLESCENCE

For most identity theorists, identity formation and the time of youth go hand in hand. It is the last and concluding stage of childhood, and childhood is completed only when childhood tags which tell him who he is are vanished and are subordinated by this new time of youth achieved in a social and competitive apprenticeship with peers.

Many youth reflect this tension and quest for identity. As the adolescent context for religious conversion reflects the same thing, many look for the "right choice" now in these adolescent years. Like the Shakespearian Hamlet, the answer to the famous "to be or not to be" reflects youth's concerns. Hamlet can be pictured as the normal, introspective youth trying to sort out life, free from his parents, facing a larger framework of ideology not yet his own. Hamlet believes that in his choices he will form the past and the future. Here is a man caught in an identity crisis conditioned by his age. The age of youth is ripe for indoctrination of young adults.[35]

As new ideologies come which pose values, youth's mind is organizing them. It is commonly thought that three factors influence ideological choice—opportunity, leadership, and friendship; all these are available during youth. Drives which are being unleashed in youth strive for an order. An opportunity must be made for the ideological choice to be given. Leadership must help give presence and credibility to the ideological choice. Close friendships and ties should be there for new ideologies to be formed. For this reason, if identity confusion exists, some striving for order and harmony is inevitable.

In the religious development of youth, as in the formation of personal identity, some sense of history is, as well, important. The call to return to one's "roots" so to speak, in conversional change, parallels the need in personal identity formation for a place where one is significant in time. In religion, becoming a part of God's "plan" meets this function in identity. When youth find their place in time, life becomes relevant again. Knowing where one fits historically and personally are crucial to a growing knowledge of who I am. Even though in this age this historic concern is evident, there is at the same time confusion and indecision about one's real place in history. This sorting out becomes a byproduct of the identity confrontation, as does this sorting out become a byproduct of the conversional change.

There is for youth a quest innate in adolescence, a "search for a new and yet a reliable identity" and is manifested in his endeavor to find, define, overdefine, and redefine himself and others through ruthless comparison, coupled with the quest to test the newest possibilities in all areas and to challenge the oldest in values. Role confusion takes place only when the resulting self-definition becomes difficult and the youth counterpoints rather than synthesizes his sexual, ethical, occupational, and typological alternatives and is often driven to decide definitely and totally for one side or for the other.[36]

Inner identity is important for youth, and this is when he has feelings of wholeness and progressive continuity. Perhaps in this inner identity one finds his closest kinship with the actual phenomenon of religious conversion, itself, for through it wholeness and progressive continuity become a key factor in uniting to the family of God.

Erikson's graphic description is appropriate to describe this mood. He likens this time of youth to a natural uprootedness in human life. Like a trapeze artist, "The young person finds himself in vigorous motion. He must let go of his safety hold on childhood and find himself reaching out for a firmer grasp on adulthood, depending for a breathless interval on the relation between the past and future, on the reliability of those that he must let go of, and reach out to those whom he feels may receive him."[37]

Adolescence is a time, then, for searching, seeking answers to identity itself, a time of major crisis of identity in the concluding stages of childhood. It is a time favorable for indoctrination and for the ascendency of drives—sexual as well as ideological. Adolescence is a time for historical irreversibility which may lead to a standing off and a questioning of history. It is a time for finding a reliable identity through synthesis of occupation and ethical choices. Adolescence provides a search for wholeness, totality, and progressive continuity as well as to the answers and questions of normal uprootedness in the life of the youth. But along with this, in the identity quest is a need for an ideological stance that provides answers to existential questions, the real questions that plague the time of adolescence.

RELATIONAL OBSERVATIONS

These two experiences, religious conversion and personal identity, have a unique relationship. People change after religious conversion experience, and people change after finding out who they are in the experiencing and sensing of their own identities. One might say, then, that religious conversion experience and identity experience are alike, even perhaps the very same in experience, in fact. All religious conversions have as a chief component identity concerns. Not all identity experiences are obviously religious in nature, however, but religious conversion in experience is an identity experience. It is this way because both the experience of religious conversion and identity are centrally associated with change in the lives of individuals. Both experiences are concerned with the changing of behavior and with the result of a changed frame of reference. Ethical implications follow changed mental constructs. These two experiences affect the very center of awareness in an individual. Religious conversion accomplishes this through a basic change of viewpoint and a forthcoming commitment to a "way" or ideology. Personal identity experiences succeed through the successful resolution of crises and the resultant virtue and values formed in the process, through interaction with individuals and society and its norms. The result of both experiences is that of a changed life at the center of one's life. Religious conversional change finds man in a new "way," when he "fits" in God's plan, and identity change is in the experiencing of a new sense of integrity by knowing one has chosen right and is complete. He perceives its "rightness" through the mirrors of others in role response. The former may proceed from the latter.

Religious conversion has a deep, integrating effect and influence on the personal attitudes, values, and feelings about oneself. Personal identity experiences likewise integrate feelings of wholeness and sameness in individuals. In religious conversion, this sense of integration comes at the resolution of the crises conflict, or the postconversion stage of the conversion crisis. In identity experience, it seems to come, I believe, through the resolution of the crisis of identity itself. Identity experience appears to be the strongest when there is opportunity for strong, even life-involving decisions, and in religious conversion as well there is a laying on the line of the life at a crossroads-type decision-making event or choice. This integrating, ultimate, focusing experience is innate to both experiences and gives direction for the future role and beliefs of the young person.

Religious conversion and identity deal with issues similar in nature. For example, religious conversion provides a sense of trustworthiness by suggesting an ultimate "One" or "way" in whom or in which one can rely; it then provides autonomy in making the decision for change itself; it seems to establish initiative by allowing freedom of personal choice among peers; it fosters identity through community and personal goals; and it cultivates integrity by developing faith in someone outside yourself.

While identity experience stresses integration of life with the world, the religious traditions indicate that wholeness and completeness come in community with the world. The one who seeks God finds complete rest and wholeness in the knowledge that God is his God, and the peace and reconciliation which come from knowing this provides the religious motivation in the world. The community of the saints so pictured in I Corinthians 11 and onward suggests that the body of believers has a purpose. The purpose is to be a model of "God-disclosure" as the expression of one's belonging to the Body of Christ. Each one is an essential part of the whole united body of Jesus. So as the youth or adult finds himself through the identity experience or through the biblical model of identity—religious conversion—and as the New Birth occurs and men and women are given spiritual capacities, the community becomes the major place pronouncing one "fit," thus giving personal identity through association, acceptance, and support. This acceptance leads to action and the Christian mission. Churches which fail to see the importance of this personal identity function for their ministry miss the great personal value of the church itself in the twentieth century.

Religious conversion has a primary relationship with the deep issues which encourage identity. It is not a relationship in the actual time-history, but in the type of issues that it can deal with. Erik Erikson suggested that one does not successfully move through to the next identity issue and therefore to a healthy identity unless one successfully deals with the various stage-ascendancy issues. This is important in the relationship to religious conversion, for with the latter experience in a moment of thorough, gradual decision making, one may rework through the previous unsuccessful stages and emerge on the positive side completely.

Both experiences have roots within the conflicts of adolescence, as well, and therefore role experimentation too. Adolescent role taking and rejecting of roles allows for rapid change of viewpoints and provides for increased conflictual situations. Since adolescence is a major time when identity conflicts, frustrations, and change take place most rapidly because of the environmental, psychological, emotional, and cultural development issues of the time, I believe that the same parallels and factors are widened in religious conversion. It is in youth that the first questions are encountered regarding ultimates in life, and the concern for personal future begins. These questions find answers in both religious conversion and identity questing. Experimentation in roles and ideology becomes prominent in this period, as we have mentioned, and allows for observation and acceptance of new world views; a resolution for the ideological and role confusion is found through religious conversion and in resolution of identity crisis problems. At this time, issues must be resolved regarding a meaningful future, solutions which these experiences provide. A unique intensity of emotions is apparent in this same time of crisis due to genetic, environmental, and societal pressures. Change at this time often occurs at a rapid pace.

Since personal identity rests on the foundation of trust, autonomy, initiative, role modeling, a coherent sense of self, etc., the identity crisis becomes a normal experience in adolescence and here intersects with the growing ideology of a youth. Since the identity crisis in adolescence, and even perhaps we might add the midlife crisis during the adult years, are trying times for ideological confusion to become clarified in these individuals' lives, it would seem that both these identity periods would be ripe periods for religious conversion to take place. Studies on church growth seem to even suggest this. Individuals who leave religious organizations after having been converted to them seldom return to them during the very first years. Their reasons for staying away seem to be too obvious, perhaps, and they have not had time to restructure their own ideological frameworks. However, after fifteen or so years, many come back to their original belief systems, many during the midlife time of crisis and sorting out of life goals. New ideology is being formed then, and, therefore, new chance for change occurs.[38]

The religious conversion experience and the crisis experience of identity both have this important feeling tone and crisis sense. Crisis feelings include a sense of dividedness, disunity, and increased tension. As with any decision state, there is a certain amount of anxious unrest before the resolution. In identity crisis, however, there is a unique difference, which suggests as well that identity experiences do not have to be necessarily religious in nature. There is in identity experience no sense of sin, per se, during the confusions and tensions, unless there is a precursor to the experience, shame and guilt from inner problems. As the two actual experiences blend in religious conversion experience, sin and salvation, good and evil, shame and sinfulness, freedom and joy all participate in the crisis resolution. The similar feeling tones of the two experiences, that of positive resolution, with its sense of unity, organization, and postdisaster utopia, suggest the identity function in religious conversion. Through this religious identity experience, life has new meaning, direction, and purpose, and the individual experiencing religious-identity-conversion has a new place in life-history—yes, even salvation history, through his return and choice to come back to God.

In identity experience and religious conversion experience there is an intensity of feelings toward commitment. The identity function of religious conversion experience sends the individual through strong feelings of anxiety or confusion, of giving up, or surrender to ultimates. After the crisis is over, tension is released and feelings of unity are begun. The resulting sense of commitment is usually to something new. For identity experience alone, it may be in the form of an intensely committed belief in oneself, while in religious-identity-conversions, commitment to God is produced. The deep commitment is extant in both.

When we look at the two experiences themselves, both are framed, molded, and shaped by the actual manifestation of conflict and tension. These factors always exist in the midst of crises. The question being resolved aids in the magnitude of the experience itself. "Who am I?" "Where am I going?" and "What is there in life for me?" are existential questions and are fraught with contending conflicts and tension. These questions themselves are the kind that fashion turning points in one's life. These questions provide movement toward maturity and the answers to these become identity tags in the movement toward God. There is, however, slight similarity in the way extreme identity experience and acute religious conversion experience are physically manifested. The physical manifestations that accompany religious conversion experiences do not seem to be duplicated in most identity crises. When the identity crisis takes the shape of conversion specifically, then there are similarities, for the experience is a part of each.

Religious conversion and personal identity experience deal with existential questions. Yet religious conversion, even though usually framed in a more open religious context since it is a decision for God in a sense, provides the same kinds of anchorages that positive resolution of identity questions provide. These answers sometimes seem to be accompanied with struggles and intense anguish.

Religious conversion may become a more negative identity decision for some, or a kind of retreat for others. Since the formation of a negative identity is a means of resolving the confusion of identity in negative terms, in order for conversion to be a negative function of identity its content must contain those identities that are the opposite of that which the youth wants to become or was told to become. This is probably not a genuine religious conversion, but perhaps we could call it counter-conversion, implying that it is not a positive thing but is brought about by manipulation and impulse; it is a reaction rather than a choice made to respond to inner needs or the pleading of an ultimate Being. This also takes into account that some religious conversions are easily explained through the external causes, through the experience of reaction, pressure, revivalism, emotionalism, or peer pressure. These may not provide lasting answers to the questions of life and identity. This does not in any way imply that a change does not occur, but change is not evidence of genuineness; it is simply a validation that movement has taken place within the center of a person's being. For religious conversion to be a negative identity there must be an incomplete understanding of one's identity. There may even be a kind of pathology or a high tendency toward suggestion present in this counter-conversion. As suggested here, conversion relates more favorably with identity formation than with negative identity formation. The possibility exists, however, for religious conversions to function in a way as to be a reaction against rather than a movement toward something. And since conversion is being viewed as a means of solving intense identity-like conflict, the possibility also exists for it to evidence itself as a negative identity, probably, for some cases.

Religious conversion could even be a kind of identity moratorium for some, if we want to use identity language. It may provide a time for the youth or the adult, for that matter, to experiment with ideological directions and their implied role definitions. For religious conversion to be part of a moratorium it must be viewed not so much as a movement and an experience as a commitment to an ideology or intensely-held position. This, you remember, is a part of our working definition for religious conversion. It is in this respect that moratorium of conversion provides basic decisions for life, yet allows time after the basic commitment to God for possible role determinations and experimentation. Eventually, however, the role will become plain and the youth will continue to mature. Religious conversion viewed in its longitudinal effects, that of occurring over a long period of time, has a much closer relationship here than conversion viewed in its rapid form and decisional aspect.

The actual functional relationships of religious conversion to identity formation are many. There exists in these two experiences a relationship as to the service they provide to the emerging individual and again suggest the identity nature of religious conversion. The functions that exist for these experiences are observable. For example, each experience provides through resolution or decision many of the same products in the life.

Through religious conversion a sense of faith is established, due to the faith-leap of the convert. Something or someone outside himself is presented as being available, and hope is encouraged. Religious conversion has implicit within its nature an ideological framework and integral to this framework is "hope." By accepting the others as being able to sustain you and solve the dilemmas of life, hope becomes a factor of consciousness.

The products of identity resolution have religious overtones. Hope is nourished by faith generated in conversion's decision to trust in God. Purpose is nourished through the play of childhood and the decisions of adults from conversion. The individual finds in accepting and yielding to the experience a purpose in life from the unifying nature of the occurrence itself. Erik Erikson's fidelity, as one of the virtues and products of identity formation, finds reinforcement in conversion, when the decision made in religious conversion allows for new loyalties, freely pledged, in view of alternative and contradictory value systems. The intensity of commitment usually accompanying the conversion strengthens feelings of fidelity. The biblical concept of love is shown in the community of faith provided by these as the new convert joins for fellowship. Here sharing is developed as an additional strength seen in identity as well. Care is in the conversion experience through the totality of change and the concomitant ideological framework, which usually is religious and probably is humanitarian.

Wisdom, that detached concern with life itself in the face of death, is planted through commitment in conversion. Religious conversions commit one to a direction, to a grappling with existential questions whose answers promote wisdom and peace in later life or old age.

In addition to the above function, the experiences are alike and must be viewed as blended in that both religious conversion and personal identity experiences allow self-certainty to be developed through role experimentation. The one undergoing religious conversion finds a new role for himself; it is different in its demands. Religious conversion experience produces identity itself, then, and it is perhaps here that we find its closest relationship.

A major role in the religious conversion experience that cannot be overlooked is its function in identity formation itself. The religious conversion experience is a calling to something new, something reorganizing and integrating in a deep level of consciousness. Conversion causes heightened awareness and acute perceptions to a sense of danger of the self; therefore, a heightened coping activity within the mind ensues. It causes a desperate search for resources by which to meet the needs so vividly experienced with the sole purpose of providing a new person with the qualities of newness (new ideologies, new perceptions, new achievements, new commitments). Religious conversion experience brings to a sharp focus a person's role in situations of crisis and awakens and mobilizes resources for resolution of the tension produced through perceived senses of sin. Religious conversion provides a new and unusual opportunity to deal with life in a fresh and creative way, and therefore the religious conversion experience has as its prime function a resultant sense of wholeness and continuity with life. This is an obvious correlation with the identity theories. It may provide a group identity and even an historical identity, if the experience comes with a supporting group. This is a functional task of identity in its secular usage itself.

It is possible that conversion functions in terms of the ego processes, too. Since the ego functions as a regulator and guide to the crisis experience and is at the core of the decisions and their resolutions by providing sameness, integrity, and continuity through change, so religious conversion functions as a regulator to resolve conflict and provide continuity and congruity. Both experiences seem to make use of this function of the ego. Granted, religious conversion includes an element of the supernatural working through the natural process, but this aspect is hard to observe and probably even harder to explain or understand.

Religious conversion, as identity, fills the intense need for devotion. It is this aspect of this identity crisis and conversion which forms the basic drive toward establishing a meaningful world view. This need for devotion in individuals allows ideologies which promote devotion to play major roles in determining later identity and provides the content for its formation itself. Ideologies offer to the member of age groups simple but determined answers to those vague questions caused by both experiences and crisis and conflict. The religious identity experience of conversion is a fulfiller of this ideological sense.

Personal identity experience, then, is a context for faith. Religious conversion as an identity-forming experience provides the moment for faith to begin. Why people choose God in religious conversion is hard to explain, but at least one such reason is that in religion is an answer to life's questions. And since we are postulating that religious conversion experience is a means for experiencing personal identity, the factors that influence identity as well influence conversion.

Society and culture have impact on the way struggle for identity is perceived, much like the religious society and religious culture prepare youth for religious resolutions to life's problems in conversion. For example, common patterns of upbringing that are acceptable in one particular culture may produce individuals who have shared specific areas of vulnerability, which predict certain kinds of identity formation. Religious conversion, likewise, is seen to be influenced by culture, group pressure, revivalism, even by possible personality correlates which make for susceptibility. Religious conversion, you will remember, occurs most often in the context of groups and in those with low ego strengths. For those whom religious conversion can readily be traced to vulnerability, there may even be a correlation between failure to successfully fulfill the crisis stages of identity formation and then experience a religious conversion as a counter-conversion or a form of negative identity.

In addition to cultural and societal influences that shape the experience, there can be added psychological, emotional, and developmental contexts for both experiences. The same factors that aid in successfully completing the epigenetic cycle for Erikson could well be operating in the religious conversion experience, too. For example, peer pressure, group identity, societal norms, and an adult guarantor's suggestions and influence would have a positive or even a negative correlation to the nature of the experience in the same way each of these influence inner and outer change in the lives of individuals through identity.

It would appear that there is a primary relationship, then, between the contexts of both experiences as they appear in the developmental, emotional, psychological, and societal milieu of life. There are obvious areas, however, where no relationships can be observed in these two experiences, and only tertiary similarities can be postulated. For example, I believe that conversion cannot be totally equated with identity experience, partly due to the limitations of the definitions themselves. Religious conversion stresses a specific moment or decisive time of change. Personal identity experience has been suggested as being a process beginning with birth and ending at the time of death. Adolescence and youth are prime ages for intense struggle and resolution of many identity conflicts and so during this time religious conversion as an identity function may occur. If identity is seen as a lifelong process, largely unconscious to the individual and his society unless a more radical confusion or negative identity or moratorium occur, it has its closest relationship, then, in the more gradual form of religious conversional change, whose changes in the life of religious nature happen almost imperceptibly with periods of incubation. In this context religious conversion would have a close relationship. Here then is the obvious contrast. Religious conversion tends to show up more often in the form of a crisis moment with rapid resolution and is like the crisis of identity experience, but not like the process of identity formation itself. Therefore, religious conversion is a means of acquiring an identity, but not the identity process per se, only one small part of it.

The identity experience is subtle and unconscious at

times; when the crisis and confusional states of identity are more openly felt and resolved, there is a more open parallel with conversion. Yet one cannot eliminate the real sense of "religious" always present in religious conversion. The presence of the "holy" is significant for conversion to be meaningful; without this it becomes just an identity experience. Perhaps the differences are as significant as the similarities in this case. Only if through the intense struggle of identity formation would the participant in this struggle attach some subjective religious quality to the experience could an identity experience be construed to be totally equated with religious conversion experience. A person going through this kind of experience attaches meaning of a religious nature to it. He would do better to change his so-called identity struggle to the religious conversion struggle to eliminate definitional confusion. Conversion must therefore be thought of as being a kind of identity experience. It is safe, then, to suggest, I believe, that all conversion experiences are identity-related, but not all identity experiences are, obviously, religious conversion. Religious conversion is a subheading for identity in this specialized sense.

What can be concluded, then, is first, religious conversion experiences and identity crisis experiences involving a resolution of the crisis constitute a means whereby individuals may radically change at a deep and meaningful level. These changes affect the basic self, for they affect ideology, behavior, and ego processes which are the core of a person's being.

Second, there are many functional relationships between religious conversion and personal identity formation in the areas of ego strength genesis, identity formation itself, ego processes, ideological satisfactions, and role experimentation.

Third, in the constituent dynamics of religious conversion and personal identity crises experiences, similar relationships exist as to the fundamental nature of the crisis experienced. These include similarities in the general feeling tones, constructs of the crisis, content of the crisis, decision, and the obvious resultant functions of integration and congruity.

Fourth, regarding the context of both, parallels exist which verify the assumptions posed. The religious conversion identity aspect finds a similar context in developmental and emotional needs fulfillment. The ascendancy of adolescence in both experiences is most significant. Both experiences deal with need satisfaction, age, problem orientation, and maturational context during the troubled time of questing.

This identity quality of the religious conversional change hints at the importance of recognizing that knowing God in a personal way through the process of religious conversion is identity producing. Personal identity is a beautiful biblical theme. God works through his people "called by name" to be used in the task of revealing God's character to the world. Churches, synagogues, parishes, and fellowship groups cluster around a common identity. Interaction within and through the fellow travelers focuses identity, sustains it, gives it a purpose and a coherence in life. The apostle Paul suggested a boldness that allows the one "in Christ" to come into the very presence of God himself. The confrontation for those with hope and trust and a sense of oneness with God would be fraught with fear and dread without this new-found identity with God. Yet we enter into God's presence in the New Testament because God has given us a way to God. His identity is ours now through his death. The Christian world can now approach God.

NOTES

1. Erik Erikson, "Identity and the Life Cycle," *Psychological Issues*, I, No. 1 (New York: International Universities Press, Inc., 1959), p. 142; see also Erik Erikson, *Young Man Luther* (New York: W. W. Norton and Co., 1959), p. 22.

2. Erik Erikson, *Insight and Responsibility*, (New York: W. W. Norton and Co., 1964), p. 153.

3. Erikson, *Young Man Luther*, p. 118.

4. Ibid., p. 21.

5. Erikson, *Insight and Responsibility*, p. 155.

6. Ibid., p. 127.

7. Erikson, *Young Man Luther*, pp. 92–94.

8. Ibid., p. 93.

9. Ibid., p. 94.

10. Ibid.

11. Ibid., p. 93.

12. Erikson, *Insight and Responsibility*, p. 140.

13. Erikson illustrates this face-to-face relationship in his analysis of a youth who was among a small group of patients who came from theological seminaries. This youth had developed symptoms while attending a Protestant seminary in the Middle West where he was training for missionary work in Asia. He had not found the expected transformation in prayer; he needed to see God to validate his direction. The need was manifested by an anxiety dream in which a face horribly unrecognizable thus seemed to echo, according to Erikson, his patient's religious scruples. Erikson diagnosed the man as troubled and with a desire to see God in order to provide him an identity. This need for divine recognition may be at the base of some conversion experiences. See Erikson, *Insight and Responsibility*, p. 65.

14. Erikson, *Young Man Luther*, p. 14.

15. Gordon W. Allport, "Crises in Normal Personality Development," *Contemporary Adolescence: Readings*, ed. by Hershel D. Thornburg (Belmont, Calif.: Brooks/Cole Publishing Company, 1971), p. 394.

16. Erikson, *Insight and Responsibility*, p. 138.

17. Erikson, *Identity: Youth and Crises*, p. 40.

18. Erikson, *Young Man Luther,* pp. 41–45.
19. Ibid., p. 42.
20. Ibid.
21. Ibid., p. 14.
22. Ibid., pp. 2–39.
23. Allport, "Crises in Normal Personality Development," p. 396.
24. Erik Erikson, *Gandhi's Truth,* (New York: W. W. Norton and Co., Inc., 1969), p. 47.
25. Erikson, *Insight and Responsibility,* p. 95.
26. Erikson, *Young Man Luther,* p. 38.
27. Ibid., p. 43.
28. Erik Erikson, ed., *The Challenge of Youth* (New York: Doubleday and Co., Inc., 1963), p. 10.
29. Erikson, "Identity and the Life Cycle," p. 111.
30. Ibid., p. 111–112.
31. Orrin E. Klapp, *Collective Search for Identity* (New York: Holt, Rinehart and Winston, Inc., 1969), p. 44.
32. Erikson, *Identity: Youth and Crises,* p. 176.
33. Jere Yates, "Erikson's Study of the Identity Crisis in Adolescence and Its Implications for Religious Education" (Ph.D. dissertation, Boston University, 1968), p. 123.
34. Erikson, "Identity and the Life Cycle," p. 123.
35. Kenneth Keniston, *Youth and Dissent: The Rise of a New Opposition* (New York: Harcort Brace Jovanovich, Inc., 1960), pp. 3–27.
36. Erikson, *Insight and Responsibility,* p. 92.
37. Ibid., p. 90.
38. Research done in church growth patterns conducted during 1977–78 in the Southeastern California Conference of Seventh-Day Adventists.

CHAPTER VI

IDENTITY: Conversion and Religious Instruction

> "Man is not liberated from his old nature by impera-
> tives to be new and to change, but he rejoices in the
> new which makes him free and lifts him beyond him-
> self. Where repentance is understood as a spiritual re-
> turn to the evil and rejected past, it deals in self-
> accusation, contrition, sackcloth and ashes. But when
> repentance is a return to the future, it becomes con-
> crete in rejoicing, in new self-confidence, and in
> Love." Jürgen Moltmann.

Often we think of becoming ourselves, becoming whole,
or even finding ourselves in some mystical way. The process of change, through religious conversion with its religious motivation or through identity with a more secular
source—or a seemingly secular one—the change process is
one which gives new meaning to life. It reaches out beyond
the now and points to the future, as Moltmann suggests.
Often, however, we live only in the nowness of our own
lives. Personal identity and religious conversion as experiences force us out of ourselves to see the way to go, the
beliefs to believe, the fit of life.

Guiding individuals to find God is a most complex task
and very difficult, and teachers of religious values have
been confronted with a task most complex in itself, confused in its content and little understood in its process.

The outcome of religion, of course, is change, and it is a purpose implicit within the religious educator's task. Change in movement and in life toward God himself is the outward purpose. The religious educator has, however, a number of factors in his favor as he begins his educational/ theological task, especially when it comes to the specific task of aiding change and growth in religious values.

The religious educator is working with individuals who are seeking identity. The movement in these lives is toward an authentic self, validated by others—society, church, home, and the world. Men and women are on a pilgrimage, often little perceived, yet nevertheless real, a quest, a search for the realness of personhood. The quest innate in man can be built upon by the religious educator. It seems logical, then, to look at the obvious implications for those engaged in the process of Christian nurture and faith genesis.

The process of religious education is difficult to clarify, as already mentioned. According to Lewis Sherrill, it "is the attempt, ordinarily by members of the Christian community, to participate in and to guide the changes which take place in persons in their relationships with God, with the church, with other persons, with the physical world and with oneself."[1] This type of education is defined by the unique type of content and process born of the tradition involved in the lives of youth.

Like William Williamson, I once believed religious education to be a very easy subject to talk about—simply a process whereby the learner of any age is taught in the setting of the Christian faith. I now realize this simplistic approach is naive, if not presumptuous.[2] To understand the process of religious education is to understand the nature of the atonement. St. Paul himself simply uses pictures to describe it. In allusions to its forensic nature, he suggests that it is like a law court, a slave market, and a temple.[3] The process is supernatural, the direction is redemptive and freeing. Religious education is a process like that. It can be defined in the same theological context as atonement, for its purposes and goals are equal. Just as the process of ministerial training is to instruct in the skills and tools and theology to enable God's people to be instruments in dispensing God's grace to a lost/saved world, so the ministry of the religious educator is to enable him as well to dispense God's grace within an educational setting, be it the church, parish, or schoolroom. This enabling process requires religious conversion, reorganization of self, new content and methods, just as any other kind of education does. At this point, I could begin a long defense and definition of educational setting, but that would be to bypass the main purpose of this chapter. In this brief suggestion I only want to remind us that learning takes place everywhere, and the educational setting for religion cannot be limited to the school, church, home, Sunday School, pastor's study, youth program, or local fellowship. Religious education's primary function involves the whole of life, itself, and in life religious educational concerns and religious identity and personal identity concerns come to the front. Williamson concludes, however, that the only answer to religious education and trying to define it is that "Christian groups do organize their resources and theologies and personnel for an activity or program often described as instruction in content material selected as important and relevant to the particular Christian group, with appropriate methods and for purposes and ends designated by the group."[4] Therefore, religious education includes indoctrination, but in addition it includes the process of life change. One must assimilate its tenets internally and it has within its methodology implicit freedom to choose positions, for through indoctrination may come commitment, but only if presented in the light of God's free love. So, while listing the aims of this process, certain theological priorities come to the front. First of all, actual growth in the church is an important by-product of the religious educational task. Developing in persons the capability for religious responses to life and enhancing the divine/human encounter as well as explanation of religious truth become key goals. All of these issues find some kind of focus in religious conversion experience and identity function, as well. How, then, does understanding this close relationship of identity formation and religious conversion experience affect the teacher-learner-God problem?

QUESTOR-GUIDE RELATIONSHIP

There is a bipolar relationship which exists between the learner and the teacher in that two results are desired— religious conversion and positive identity formation. Identity issues which surface have religious significance and are grappled with in a context of a community of individuals whose values become instrumental in leading a growing person through acceptable and confirming roles.

The student should be understood as questor. Eager expectation about the life of faith can be validated by a community of faith. Since religious conversional change as identity experience is supported by what is perceived and expected in the roles that are chosen, close attention must be given to the selection of the guides whose encounters with questors of identity will be validating and affirming. Encounter situations should be a concern for the body of believers, then, for as the youth engage with adults whose identity is secure, within this encounter the perceived values will enhance their conversional change and verify the church's meaning.

Concern for the inner identity needs by leaders will aid in this process of change. Religious conversion experience as an identity anchorage can be understood only through teachers who fully comprehend the experiences the youth are going through during their crises.

Since religious conversion seems to be an experience which, through manipulation and coercion, may lead to a negative identity, it would be well for leaders and youth to function together as units, sharing roles and experiences of faith and understanding mutual identities, rather than adults trying to manipulate youth to accomplish conversions or to "have" an experience.

One important task for the church which would take into account the importance of this relationship in religious growth is to encourage an *intergenerational context for faith building*. When all generations can share in the interchange of Christian ideas, responsibility, and worship, the symbolic meanings of faith become relevant to the questor—through his guide.

Therefore, it would seem in this intergenerational context, more effective teaching of the values of religion in life and society would be done. By realizing the identity potential of man's return to God in religious conversion, the church family creates an atmosphere of trust, hope, value, faith, and even trustworthiness. Youth would, I believe, be more free to select the direction for their lives rather than to experience counter-conversion and a possible negative identity reaction.

Although we often attribute our insistence that others "become converted" to a Christian "love," unless the questor perceives that we respect individual creativity and freedom, I believe problems will result. As a result of this kind of open, intergenerational experience, *creativity* would emerge in the local educational setting of the church. Creativity is an expression of freedom, an expression of an individual finding his own way, so necessary to relating to God.

Many students would like to try new things and be creative but sense an aura of disapproval from adults who view this creativity as "obstreperousness" or "rebellion," because the creativity may result in something "different." Even though the goal is to develop creativity from the basis of freedom, often teachers feel threatened by these divergent thinkers, and creativity is hampered. Many educators may agree that individuality is desirable and even express the necessity for it, yet when it actually takes place (for example, in a religion class by a challenging new exegesis, or a new method of evangelism) we, as teachers rather than as guides, feel threatened by the directness and new insight that this creative person insists upon showing. It is a strange paradox, indeed. When one seeks for God in the life and makes a free response, he is able then to choose and return to him; yet we often stifle the freedom to choose by coercion and mold the setting wherein the choice is to be made. When creativity does show up, it differs in style or arrangement from what our typical views are. Charges of heresy are often shouted, as we ourselves fear a challenge to our position. Youth perceive it as suppression of personal identity and individuality.

Oftentimes youth view the religious educator as another parent. The questors see themselves in a kind of supremacy game with the educator, trying to achieve personal identity and answer the question of "Who is in charge here?" However, with this concept prevalent in some youths' minds, the teacher who fails to guide and be sensitive to the quest in progress closes the door to an identity resolution or even to a commitment in religious conversion. So often the teacher verifies who is really in charge and holds the authority in this particular class setting. There will be no doubt in youths' mind just what they must do or learn in order to beat the system and emerge victorious, for the teacher will let it be known who is the fount of truth. A pseudo-intellectual guessing game ensues with the youth trying to guess his identity by proper questions and answers. Adults leading individuals towards free identity choices must concern themselves with some of the following issues. Good intergenerational approaches which foster creativity must include

1) *Openness for questioning.* One of Christ's greatest teaching devices was the honest question. An atmosphere of freedom existed for people to approach Jesus to question him regarding his own mission and message. Earnest seekers after truth must feel open to express frank and deep questions. Creative questions may be the springboard to great truths otherwise left unexplored and permanent decisions to change.

2) Religious educators must in the relationship *reflect the God they too seek,* rather than direct the focus to themselves. This approach will eliminate the ego-tripping of many religious educators who promote their own views as the only truth to be grasped.

3) *Avoidance of "preaching the truth"* to youth will result in individuals who have found truth for themselves. Exploration of religious literature will be invited rather than prescribed; therefore, the truth perceived by the young questor in identity formation will be his truth, and his personal faith will begin to emerge.

4) Intergenerational workers will *listen to counter arguments* and facts without fear of losing the identity seeker. A social psychological experiment done in 1949 by Lumsdaine

and Sheffield showed that when a belief is so widespread in a society that various individuals have no opportunity to encounter contradictory evidence or opinion, the belief will yield to strong persuasive attacks at a much later date. This is because the individuals have no occasion to develop resistance to counter-attack. The principle can apply to our work with youth in the identity quest.

Youth respect sound arguments from guarantors who know their beliefs and respect personal commitments but will learn in a more committed way when they are able to be themselves and ask their own questions. As Paul Irwin suggests, "The church fails its youth if it lacks spirit, but it fails them equally if it does not encourage the discipline of critical thought in shaping a vision of life that can provide intelligent direction."[5] It would seem that more effective teaching of values of religion and society could be done by realizing the identity potential of the conversion experience and by providing an atmosphere of trust, hope, and fidelity in which youth could select the direction of their lives rather than to cause counter-conversion, as we have called it, and force youth into a possible negative identity.

Adults in their relationships with youth should also provide proper moratoria for role experimentation itself. If the experience of conversion becomes a possible moratorium from dealing with the issues of living in this negative sense, adults should respect this aspect of the religious conversion process.

Since historical processes are vitally related to the demand for personal identity in each new generation, and since religious conversion experience is a means of entering into the collective community of faith in a given tradition, proper, clear, and determined understandings of the historical perspectives of a personal role and place in history and a collective role in society will aid in avoiding identity crises based on failure to know where one fits "in the scheme of things." Religious conversions—turning or returning to—would be easier if a clear understanding of this historical sense would be elucidated by leaders in the church and school. Relationships are crucial: "The anthropological condition of religion is to be found in the 'dialectics' of individuals and society that pervade the processes in which consciousness and conscious are individuated."[6] Again in this dialectic, we affirm regularized status passages or "coaching relationships" which build new bridges in identity.[7]

IDENTITY, CONVERSION, AND CONTENT

There are implications in this close association of religious conversion and the crisis of identity for those who design curriculum materials and are concerned with the actual content of religious learning. It is important here to define content in its most broad sense, perhaps using James Michael Lee's definition which includes the actual process of education as content itself. This kind of content must thoroughly reflect analysis of the emotional forces that the contents engender in the lives of those with whom educators come in contact. The material content itself should include a view of the personal, individual problems of youth so they will be facing a face rather than merely facing a problem.[8] An awareness of the conflicts that cause experience to be expressed are important here.

Resolution of the conversion crisis of identity will, as mentioned before, generate values as a product of the experience. One primary function of religion is that of value genesis. People who know where they fit and who have a new ideology within God's family have a new hierarchy of values, it seems, which aids in the assessments and choices of life. One objective content, then, in religious experience is that of values. The test of how effective the return to God is how real one's real identity with God and his followers has become is evidenced by how well-maintained and long-kept those values are. A gradual shifting of values, a slow erosion of their motivational thrust, or a rejection of the group's values could be a measure of how deep the quality of the new religious values and identity is. When religion no longer is the progenitor of values for its adherents, the religion is idolatry or, worse, hypocrisy.

Values find sanction within the theology, culture, commitment, and values of adult guarantors as well as within the relationship with fellow pilgrims.

The religious educational setting is a primary time when this content of religious instruction is at the front. In the encounter of people moving towards God, values are prominent. If one would believe Ivan Illich, "School systems in general have as a primary focus the shaping of man's vision of reality."[9] If this is true of the so-called secular school, what depth of concern should the religious education enterprise have for developing proper values?

Since the work of the educator in religion is the direct process of guiding the development of others, it is by nature involved in value building. From the moment someone suggests the music to be listened to at an evening meeting to the method whereby discipline is meted out, religious education has the responsibility of sharing values.

Most recent major researchers in the field of value education at some time in their study refer to Philip Jacob's study done in 1957. Jacob's approach, designed to examine values and their transmission in higher education found, in brief, that no specific curriculum patterns, no model syllabus for social science, no pedigree of instructor, no wizardry of method, had much impact on values and their formation. Only two significant factors were hinted at that I believe were pertinent to our work: 1) Values changed within the distinctive climate of a few institutions; and 2) Values changed through a relationship with and the personal magnitude of sensitive teachers.[10] Research since the Jacob's report has taken two directions. Agreement with his results sent scholars in search of extracurricular influences on values. Examples of these were the home, peer groups, and value-laden experiences. These projects yielded little fruit; however, some significant findings came from those who researched peer group pressure. Changes for some students seemed to occur under this influence, with dormitory living tending to influence some negatively. This research was done in a secular environment, yet a parallel study would prove an interesting project within religious educational settings, should someone wish to pursue it.

More fruitful, however, than the peer group studies have been those pursuing Jacob's clue that a few institutions held a climate which pervaded the whole institution and thus influenced students' values most. Surely this is not just a trick of fate or something that has just happened! This "climate" is the result of planning. The facilities of schools most effective in value changing were ones united in instruction, purpose, and mission. Those with a clear sense of direction became the instigators of change in students' lives and provide the framework whereby identity can be greatly enhanced.

This is a clear call for self-appraisal, recommitment, and unity within religious educational settings. The century that found such growth in media, communication and world concerns stands speechless unless recommitment to a purpose and reevaluation of personal involvement with the mission of God become key points again in our view of the religious educational task. This value content in religion is an important concern for the religious educator.

Perhaps we have been living with the myth that because we believe intellectually in the best values, these will be passed on to those we meet, somehow, someway, by someone, sometime. Evidence seems to contradict this assumption. The process of value formation and value transmission is a project that must be incorporated in every philosophy, methodology, curriculum of school, church, and home.

In any religious education situation, then, attempts should be made toward an understanding of our purposes. It is this identity task that enhances personal religious conversion experience as identity function. At a recent school board meeting I attended, while individuals were stressing the importance of using innovative curriculum materials, a question came regarding what effective and cognitive objectives were incorporated into the board's thinking of this new material. Most either did not know the meaning of the words, or ignored altogether the relationship of method to objectives. If little time is spent in clearly understanding our common mission in the world, aimless wandering will be the result and identity will never be formed. The tragic aftermath of our meanderings will be the minimal value change within those who experience our religious educational setting.

Yet these questions can still be raised: How can a climate for learning be changed or directed? How is a climate established at all? Does one listen to the rumors in the constituency or to the natives within the compound in trying to evaluate it?

Climate direction for value learning and enhancement of the identity experience for young people is more easily assessed than believed. Some methods can include the following: 1) *Informal discussions* with students, parents, and individuals involved about specific goals for the mission of religious organizations. 2) *Retreats* with the sole function of establishing a God-given direction and reassessing the directions in the past, sharpening the religious focus on the real issues of mission. 3) *Value orientation* among various disciplines within our churches, noticing the relationship of each one's function with the other fields of study. This helps integrate religion into real life. This also helps to broaden the base for value learning, taking the sole responsibility away from the clergy, and distributing it equally to the saints. 4) A conscious *meeting for direction,* with all the individuals involved in worship, where God can minister to the school by his Spirit. 5) Any *dialogue* whereby the focus of the religious educational institution can be appointed its function in the light of its mission will assist the climate and therefore raise the value-transmitting potential. Another factor to consider in this issue is the nature of learning values themselves. For, like the learning process, values must be meaningful to be retained. The data about values cannot precede the knowledge that they are meaningful. If their meaning comes later in the learning experience, questions such as "so what" crop up. Values must be seen to be of worth to the lives of value-minded instructors and pastors with internalized goals. The philosophical discussion about where values reside—in the mind or in the act—does not need a resolution as it relates to value learning. For others simply do receive values, and those giving them must live them. The problem of personal dedication to religious principles rears its head here. The teacher who teaches about high moral worth must himself in activities be exemplary of the value or it is not transmitted.

If the experience of learning conflicts with the words that are uttered, youth has the tendency to distrust the experience and mistrust the words, and a negative identity is formed. For example, when a child first hears from his concerned parents as he braces himself for a spanking, "This will hurt me more than it does you," the child knows this for the lie that it is.[11] But better illustrated is the story John Westerhoff tells in his book, *Values for Tomorrow's Chilren,* of the teacher who, becoming frustrated because of the lack of discipline and attention, goes off into a shouting tirade so that he may maintain order and then teach about the unconditional love of God.

If values change under the direction of the personal magnitude of sensitive teachers also, then the challenge is to evaluate our own motivations for teaching and to cultivate the types of personality characteristics that tend toward sensitivity, for in value learning as it relates to identity progress, being aware of the inclinations, feelings, world view, and frustrations of each student allows sensitivity to be more readily demonstrated. Yet the characteristic of sensitivity is not one simply decided upon and then lived out; rather, sensitivity comes as one sees in others worth and potential. Lewis Sherrill, late religious educator, suggested an appropriate term for use here. It is to be the goal of religious education and religious educators. He described the word "wholth." This word points to the potential within each student for health of the entire self, plus the concepts of holiness and God. The power to become this way is the *dunamis* of God.[12] This is a worthy concept for students, yet more noble for religious educators. For, like "wholth," sensitivity is a gift of God that stems from knowing the worth of others as objects of his love, and knowing oneself in the process of sanctification. Every individual in religious education needs religion in his own heart by faith and needs to possess a true self-denying, self-sacrificing spirit.

With these concepts, the potential for value-change and identity becoming crystalized increases, since values are more clearly perceived, and as we mentioned, values are important in the actual functioning of identity. Concerns like these do not make positive values overnight. The averages get better, however, when we get closer to our goal of reaching youth with real values for life and establishing a personal identity within their return for God. A child within this type of learning experience might express his feelings about teachers as do the lines of this haiku:

> He opened life's God
> full, knowing the choice my own,
> yet holding my weak hand.[13]

Value learning becomes a real content concern for those interested in identity formation in its religious setting. Religious conversion experience and the return to God is made easier when the deep meaning of the return is seen. Its deep meaning is manifested best in the values of the people who prescribe the return to God.

A most vital content for religious education are the Scriptures themselves. Since religious education is not designed to produce a product, per se, but rather is oriented to supply what is needed for the process of growth, Scripture is to be viewed as a major resource for God's revelation of his purpose. The use of Scripture becomes crucial in light of the religious conversion-identity issue. The Bible as a revelation of God's disclosure to man can confront us with the existential questions which are the issues of identity. Youth in the midst of identity formation and at the crossroads of deciding for or against God in their lives are being confronted through Scripture with not the historical "call" of God, but with the present "call" of God. This calling forth is seen in the declaration of God's kingdom in the Old and New Testaments, and is typified in the "discipling" concept of the New Testament, specifically. God's people have historically been challenged to *become*. Scriptural passages which invite response become most useful in understanding the beckoning of God. Such stories as the exodus (Exodus 12-16), the passover story (Exodus 12-13), Mt. Sinai (Exodus 20), Daniel's stand in Babylon (Daniel 4, 5), the temptation of Jesus (Matthew 4), the healings of Christ, especially blind Bartimaeus (Mark 10), the confession of Peter (Matthew 16), the Revelation's churches (Revelation 2-3), etc., all invite youth to respond to the historical setting, yet include the invitation for their personal response.

Scripture used only to inform and clarify becomes dry and cold. But in such passages as invitations to disciple, to find one's sense of history, to commitment and to change in lifestyle, these are most useful in a ministry to those concerned with the identity issues of youth. The church's responsibility to foster religious return through conversion as an identity function is taken seriously only when church men and women themselves recognize the invitational nature of Scripture. In commenting on a religious community's use of Luke 4:1-13 (Jesus' temptations), Irwin suggests, "In the intimacy of the small sharing group they were free to identify and to examine—even if only superficially at first—their values and lifestyles. The existential thinking of such a class session is continuous with the growth experience."[14]

The material used in Scripture must be designated to enable youth to face inner conflicts that they will find in growing into the community of believers. If the material is

oriented toward the manipulation of youth or adults
through the crisis resolution, genuine religious conversion
as we have defined it will not occur. Genuine religious
conversion change is positive in outcome, resolves identity
issues, and can only be conversion in its deepest sense if it
is not preprogrammed; it comes as the person works
through his needs and encounters his conceptions of God
and identifies with that.

A warning is perhaps in order here. The leaders of the
church and church schools should be careful not to supply
an environment too conducive to change based on the obvious observable phenomena such as crying, stress, emotionalism, manipulation, etc. Change within in this context
is coercive and denies freedom and individuality which
real religious conversion and identity experience demand.
The goal is to see changed lives because of an encounter
with the God who is holy—motivated by God and not by
man.

Scriptural material, and in fact all curriculum materials,
should attempt to establish the basic ego strengths which
reflect religious values. Since personal identity is found
within value-laden experiences and choices, it is important
that the materials used in this kind of format as well generate these supreme values and beckon man to become
religious rather than to force him into a mold which he will
later wish to demolish.

Conversion, Identity, and Learning Theory

Explanations of learning theories are legion. In practice,
they simply reflect attitudes which the religious educator
holds. The concept of religious conversion as identity,
function, however, implies concern about what one does in

the learning setting. For example, teachers of religion should avoid the use of fear and threat for learning. These serve as external psychosocial conflicts for the learner and aid in a possible negative sense of identity for counter-conversion. Any approach which encourages anxiety should be avoided if that anxiety produces superficial changes and does not lead to a grappling with existential questions of life. Some people never make changes except in the midst of stress, and as we have mentioned, crisis is a key context for identity decisions itself, but anxiety for the sake of anxiety and in order to derive an obvious result is simply manipulation and coercion and must be avoided.

The teacher should view some intense anxiety experiences, however, as normal during various age periods and plan so that his approach and philosophy allow for this to occur. He should provide a means for his own faith to serve in a guiding way to guarantee to the youth what faith does in the life. It can resolve anxiety and the crises facing him. His beliefs then become basic strength for others. This aspect of the teacher as facilitator and mentor, guide if you would, is implicit in the foregoing understanding of the close relationship of these two experiences.

In addition, thoughtful planning of experiences to challenge individuals to deal with and pose answers to those "big" value-laden questions about life should be done. Resolution of these issues—through religious traditional approaches, doctrinal clarification, ritual, celebrations, etc., aid in the identity/conversion quest. Wayne Oates suggests, for example, exploring activities such as following, moratorium, striving, and taming, as possible enrichers of the identity confirmation in youth.[15] The implicit learning theory approach here suggests that people should feel free to select answers which have been guaranteed by adults who live these values.

The Christian church in its march through history with its revivals, its Jesus freaks, its staid denominations, seeks the one thing that Jesus brings. A new life, a new start, a change to make something out of the nothing which many lives evidence is the essence of religion. The knowledge of Jesus Christ in the consciousness of each individual who believes brings this peace. The order that religion brings in the life brings that peace, as well. The justification by grace, the sanctification brought through the life of Christ and his death on the cross point to an outlook on life which is redemptive in nature, communal by definition, and self-integrating through identity with God. The early church thrived on the celebration of the presence of God with man while the baptism of the saints symbolized the close identification of being with God. These Christian symbols of the Lord's Supper, baptism, confirmation, prayer, worship, celebration, fellowship, all point to a close association of the presence of God with man as he struggles in the saga of life, and can be repeated in community to enrich the identity experiences of a growing people of God. Old Testament images of pilgrimage, calling, covenant, promise, redemption serve as identity hooks for the church to move individuals toward religious conversion as identity function. Religious conversion and identity provide the experience whereby man in his quest for wholeness sorts out the real meanings of life. All things become clear when there is a purpose for living. Experiences like religious conversion and identity provide the background for the infusion of Christianity into all the world and provide a basis for motivation in the religious mission.

NOTES

1. Lewis J. Sherrill, *The Gift of Power* (New York: Macmillan Co., 1955), p. 82.

2. William Williamson, *Concepts and Language in Christian Education* (Philadelphia, Penn.: The Westminster Press, 1970), p. 32.

3. Romans 3:24–26.

4. Williamson, *Concepts and Language in Christian Education,* p. 37.

5. Paul B. Irwin, *The Care and Counseling of Youth in the Church* (Philadelphia, Penn.: Fortress Press, 1975), p. 61.

6. Thomas Luckmann, *The Invisible Religion* (New York: Macmillan Co., 1967), p. 78.

7. Anselm L. Strauss, *Mirrors and Masks, The Search for Identity* (Glencoe, Ill.: Free Press, 1959), p. 100.

8. Erik Erikson, *Young Man Luther* (New York: W. W. Norton Co., 1958), p. 17.

9. Ivan Illich, *Deschooling Society* (New York: Harrow Books, 1970), p. 68.

10. Philip Jacobs, *Changing Values in College* (New York: Harper & Row, 1957).

11. John M. Larson, "The Individual and the Learning Community," *Religious Education* (July-August, 1972), p. 274.

12. Sherrill, *The Gift of Power,* p. 22.

13. Bailey Gillespie, "Values are for People," *Journal of Adventist Education* (Dec-Jan, 1973–1974), p. 31.

14. Irwin, *The Care and Counseling of Youth in the Church,* pp. 63, 64.

15. Wayne E. Oates, *On Becoming Children of God* (Philadelphia, Penn.: The Westminster Press, 1969), p. 110.

CHAPTER VII

RELIGIOUS CONVERSION:
Identity and the Pastoral Counseling Task

". . . Well, you know, I'm very sensitive about trying to interpret that, because I think that many people have been driven from the church by seeking some classical form that their conversion took. You know, 'I remember the day! I remember the hour! I felt the power! I fell off a horse and woke up on a certain street!' I think people have been locked into a certain cataclysmic event, and people who may not have felt that way after trying often have felt that they haven't been called or that they haven't been converted. I really think that one can have high moments, but one in my judgment should never associate a convolution with a conversion." Jesse Jackson.

The identity quest within the lives of youth on their identity pilgrimage has a great effect in the interaction they have with leaders of the church as well as in their interactions with the church's members. In addition to this quest, the religious counterpart, conversion-identity, becomes the object of the unwritten agenda for church educators. Each of us involved with the religious nurture and growth of people would, I believe, like to be successful in our work. We would like to look back over a year's ministry and see some type of success in terms of individuals committed to God. We would all like to see people who, having been exposed and guided by our ministry and care as we reflect the grace of God, have accepted a God-consciousness in their lives and now are following the ethical demands, the "better way." It is this process of moving beyond acceptance of beliefs and dogmas and traditions to show a life that is lived with the sovereignty of God as the modus operandi that is the important task for religious education and the aim to which all of religious education is directed. This could succinctly be stated as its primary goal. After all, the kingdom of God in the biblical sense reflects a dual understanding, a quality of the present life which is to be lived daily by individuals involved with God as well as understanding the kingdom of God as a possible future reality.

H. Richard Niebuhr suggests we move to the "-ings" of life, the process of believing, confessing, and committing oneself to the style of Christianity.[1] This being the case, the role of guarantors of faith in the growth of religious people is vital. The concerns of identity formation and its crisis in the process, the quest for religious identity out of which religious conversion as an identity device comes, provide rich information for those who counsel individuals in the midst of their quest, whether they are in the pastorate or without. Many individuals who come for advice and support in the counseling situation are seeking clarity of vision about their own lives.

We might wish that the answers to the religious identity quest or even personal identity problems would come in an easily-formulated axiom or traditional dogma. When a person goes on his pilgrimage, his quest, his clarification of identity, he finds that identity does not come in the "form of a rose-trellised cottage, with wife and child waiting in certainty of schedule as he returns from the kind of work his father and grandfather did before him. No. His identity comes as a cloud by day and a pillar of fire by night. He goes out not knowing where he goes, not knowing when or whether he will come back."[2] Just giving out advice to individuals who are in the midst of their quest, giving prepackaged programs which provide shallow answers, will not fulfill the expectations of those whom we counsel during these questing years.

Pastoral counseling is, then, a unique challenge, and it has undergone through the years a great deal of change. Early in the history of pastoral counseling, determinism was the basic philosophical construct around which most counseling revolved. Most early pastoral counseling was deterministic in that the client was viewed as an object to be manipulated by the counselor who had the knowledge and the know-how not possessed by the client. Thus, man in the counseling action was seen reacting from the direction of an outside force in determining his own life direction.[3] Man was viewed as an object to be used. Now, it is true that the religious counselor does bring his own theological presuppositions to the counseling situation; however, such strict determinism has yielded to a more reasoned approach which includes a sensitivity to man's unique situation. More existential methods are currently being used which I believe form the basis for the identity counseling I am suggesting.

When one takes an existential position in counseling, the counselor does not eliminate his basic assumptions about man and God's interest and requirements, but he now no longer is as concerned with a system or technique as with an underlying attitude and understanding of the uniqueness of man. This existential approach to counseling reinforces man as he is—as he is becoming.

The pastor-counselor, then, needs to be asking the

"when" questions and the "why" questions to encourage discussion about the quest the growing person is undertaking. Paul Irwin suggests the use of questions which respect the individual's identity search. He gives hints to counselors in his discussion and suggests: 1) That the counselor ask questions which reflect youth's inner world and pose questions about personal interpretations of the symbolic meanings in youth's life; 2) The counselor should probe into the important relationships in which identity is formed; and, 3) He should ask questions about the feelings and attitudes of the young person and should ask himself as a counselor if he is picking up any sensitivity for these questions in the inner world of youth which reflect feelings about himself or herself; 4) The counselor must, as well, be sensitive to what stage in this life pilgrimage the questor has progressed in the process.[4]

Provocative questions which amplify the quest for identity are the most helpful instrument in the pastor-counselor's tool kit. Those undergoing return to God through religious conversion are as well aided by questions which provide clarity during their search for God. Questions such as, "What have you learned from this about your life with God?" and "How do you see yourself understanding your relationship with God?" become the crucial ones during this time. Questions which probe human destiny, such as, "How do you see God working in your life?" aid in the youth's search for a clear picture of his own life in God's hands.

Counselors agree that this search for meaning and destiny is a basic personality hunger. The sense of belonging and fit, whether it is sensed in the anxiety of not being at home in one's heart with God, or whether it is experienced in the crisis of personal identity, not knowing where one belongs at all, is not experienced in a very abstract way in the lives of young people. We've seen its presence in the life as a "... deep 'gut-level' conviction that life is trustworthy and worth the struggle in spite of its cruelty, agony, and contradictions."[5] The counselor's role must be that of helping guide and assist in the struggle, rather than giving out information in pat answers. Youth, if they hear this kind of response, will soon leave and find their own quest in a different ideology or with a different series of caring people.

Anyone who goes on a quest to determine his own sense of worth in man's and God's sight will not only be aided by suggesting clarification and movement in growth, but will be nudged along the path to God as ultimate worth. Perhaps this is why most agree that man is basically religious. If you leave man alone by himself, he will seem to construct a basic fabric of life out of which he will find some kind of meaning. Leave him alone by himself and he will create his own secular gods. Provide, however, in his life a religious framework, guided and directed towards God, and the chances of his finding answers in God are greatly increased.

Twentieth century man is no less religious than were his predecessors. St. Augustine's familiar lines are still true: "Thou has made us for Thyself and our souls are restless till they rest in Thee."[6] Whether the gods we create are so-called secular ones or whether they are religious ones, man orders his religious life and devotes attention to the things which seem to have personal worth and meaning.

The questions, then, are crucial in the counseling relationship. They must reflect and respect man's sense of worth in the sight of God. Couple with the appropriate questions the concept that the pastor who counsels has himself a deep, contagious, and continuous knowledge of his conversion and identity with God, then the relationship between the one searching and the counselor will be therapeutic and beneficial.

The questions which deal with life's destiny and one's relationship with the omnipotent God can be near the surface of our listening. Below is a journal entry by a student in her late teens, posting her religious growth. Journal entries are excellent means of understanding individual's identity quest because the conflicts in the quest are easily described. This journal is of one kept for ten weeks, and the daily entries watch a growing sense of clarity about one's purpose in life. There is here a dialogue with oneself in the midst of a quest going on about ultimate concerns.

I do a lot of things that I hate. Being a hypocrite is not what I want to be and not what I want to do, unfortunately. There are some days when I catch myself. I really try not to gossip, complain, and put people down. I have a terrible inferiority complex. I have no means of taking my aggressions out, so I displace them and have to put the blame on something that is not guilty. I'm still having doubts as to whether I can really believe in religion.

As a whole, there are so many things that you have to have blind feelings about if you believe in the Bible, Jesus, and the end of the world. Then there are facts that are supposed to be true about evolution and everything like that. I'm not really sure what I believe. Church classes have not been any big help. I don't like religion classes.

Last Friday night, Robin made the comment that if I went to church for once in my life, maybe I could find a male. (We were on the subject of boyfriends at the time.) That's another one of my basic problems—I want a boyfriend. I can't understand why this is so foremost in my goals. I have a lot of friends and my family that all love me, but I still feel so lonely. I was with all my friends two weeks ago, and I am lonely still. I am waiting for the right one to come along. It's been hard to be patient. I'm not the flirting type, and I'm like my Dad—I am definitely not a little social butterfly. I don't meet people and talk to strangers very openly and easily. I don't feel very secure with myself. I feel fat and ugly always and I don't think I'm a total blast to be around. I want to cure myself of these major trivias, and I feel that I can't trust people with my problems, and if I do, they'll think I'm dumb, so they won't listen.

I know there is a God, but where? If I can't see him, then how am I supposed to know if he's going to help me; and if he will, then how am I going to know and understand that this is what's best for me?

Even though this entry deals with the real world of a nineteen-year-old girl, it is interesting to watch the slow evolution of identity and "fit" questions. Topics like irrelevant church classes, boys, theological belief problems like Jesus, Bible, and eschatology were important. Note, however, the questing quality of the questions at the end of the journal entry. The questions are deeply theological ones in the midst of surface relevance. Often youth's quest comes to us in the way of belief problems or social problems. For example, "Tell me, Pastor, what do you think of premarital sex?" Or questions about problems in the social sphere. The preacher in all of us sees a chance to jump and make a dictum or dogma for clarification in the young child's life. Caution, however, must overrule intellect, here. Wait and listen, see if the questions are only shallow manifestations of deep identity concerns.

There is more to the counseling situation than patient/client/pastor relationships. Pastoral counseling must be done in the context of the total church. Larry Richards suggests, "Christian education then can never deal with individual life alone. Christian education has to concern itself with the processes within the body which nurture corporate and individual growth in Christ. Any Christian educational approach which focuses on either the individual or the group in exclusion of the other is bound to fall short."[7]

church are shaped by the members within the community of faith. Not only is the counselor's relationship supportive while aiding those in search of themselves and God, but the members' attitudes in the local parish are equally as significant. Since the people in the church project their expectations to others, and those in times of crisis look for expectations to be fulfilled, a church's close look at the message it is projecting may clarify the actual role performance in the questor's life. Reuel Howe suggests, "(God) speaks and acts through us, and we become the fellowship of the redeemed and the redeeming, the fellowship of the reconciled and the reconciling."[8] What the pastor provides in theory and theology, the church as faith community lives in verity and truth. What the guarantor of faith can only personally witness to, the people of God enact.

The church is entirely too loveless. It exists often solely for its own sake and provides programs which only nurture selfish introspection. The members could fill their social needs elsewhere, but since the church is convenient, either by location or by association, its membership survives in a kind of selfish vacuum. The church I see, however, is one whose vision reaches into very practice itself. Randolph Crump Miller describes such a community. "Such a community is educationally viable, for education by one definition is what happens to a person in community. There is a nurturing process that occurs through what might be called osmosis where a sense of belonging is a powerful influence."[9]

The church, then, is a type of counselor itself. The pastor which encourages this concern will, I believe, have a congregation involved with each other and have little time for theological arguments. The congregation which recognizes its role in the passages of identity will be providing the identity tags so necessary for acceptable growth toward God.

All of us proceed through regularized status passages. For youth, these are rarely recognized by the church. Entry into a "spiritual birthday," so to speak, in the conversion is little celebrated after the first event of membership or confirmation takes place. Regularized remembrance is important to youth because it reaffirms the group's interest in the quest for personhood and identity with God in religious growth. The church must pattern, then, in a tutoring relationship the necessary steps to God and reinforce by its celebration each member's acceptance and development in their growth. Along this line is the pastor's responsibility to provide information regarding vocation.

One neglected area in church responsibility is in aiding this important identity tag—the life job. Youth seeking role identity can have the crisis resolved early if the church takes this clearly theological task to heart. The word vocation implies a calling by God. What clearer identity focus is there than in one's life work? This calling implies a God-concern for the life choices of its membership. If vocational counseling is not a part of the church's responsibility, the questor may be so involved with a role crisis that a genuine return to God can't even be considered. When the church fails to provide role identifications and meaningful moratoria for youth, confusion often results. A congregation's conscious effort to provide reassessment of the tags for identity formation will encourage resolution of the identity crisis in a positive way.

The church's community testifies to ideology as well, which has meaning and elicits commitment. The church's role in developing the ideological formation is vital. The church as tutor and counselor, or the pastor as symbolic of the ideology manifest, will, through the "style of life" of the congregation and his own person, either validate and call forth positive response or offend the budding ideologist in his identity quest.

Since religious conversion is accompanied by an ideological commitment, what the church does as it learns of its mission becomes the major teacher. In workshops in Europe during the summer months, North American pastoral-types were reminded of the subtle ideological differences in the political sphere and their influence in forming solid foundations in religion. Secularism and a definite movement away from a God-minded society were replacing a church's mission because youth could not see a vitality and focus and direction within the church's ideology.

Theological thought has always been a microcosm of man's search for God. As theology was irrelevant, man in concert with his need for meaning sought a God that was real. Through orthodoxy and traditionalism, liberalism, neo-orthodoxy to existentialism, and theology of liberation, hope and joy, we can capsulate man's search for a meaningful ideology. When the redemptive fellowship of the saints of God fails to provide a climate which shows meaningful ideology, people in search of congruity in their lives, and of course in their religious commitments, will seek elsewhere. The church as comforter or the pastor as counselor must attempt to build relevance into the theological quest with a life response in the church members and a personal life of the pastor which orders properly the response that we wish to occur in the ones we guide to God.

This task of guiding the ideologies implies respect for the personal responses being made by those we counsel. Respect may very well be the greatest attribute counselors should have when dealing with identity issues. God in his love allows free response, and man who follows after God must be equally open for freedom. Religious conversion is only really understood in the context of one's free, uncoerced response to God's invitation to return. Someone who is told what he is to be like, who is urged to accept someone else's constructs ideologically, who is pushed before he is ready will only suffer a new crisis of identity when he understands this coercion. For, "as he 'casts about' restlessly through infancy, childhood, and early adolescence, he comes to feel most at ease when he knows clearly what he means to others. He or she has an identity, a place, an estimate for others . . . finding out for oneself who one is by choice is the search upon which the adolescent is thrust."[10]

There are then some specific areas which come to the front in this type of counseling and support given by the parish, itself. They are, first of all, issues involving accepting religion as a personal faith; secondly, issues involving maturity and belonging; and thirdly, issues focusing in on religious change as a key factor.

Personal Faith

A key focus during the time of identity crisis or during the stress and anxiety of the religious return in conversion is the personalizing nature of the faith itself. Faith is not an entity to be obtained; it is simply a word that describes one's response and relationship to God and the resultant trustworthiness of God which can be relied upon. For the religious person to be fully equipped to function in relation to the sovereignty of God in life and to feel at home with his relationship with God, a time of personal, individual response must be provided.

Individuals who come during the anxiety of an identity crisis of a religious nature need direction toward the leveling influence that a deep abiding trust in the consistency of God will provide. Often individuals come for help, but our discussions center in the theological clarification that well-trained scholars can provide, and yes, even enjoy providing. However, the person on his slow return to God, or even in his abrupt response to God's call, needs time for personal faith to be individualized. What the counseling relationship should provide is a safe place to hide. The concept of God in Scriptures implies this. God is seen as a rock, as a place to hide in the Old Testament. We think of a rock and we imagine a great mass of granite; our God would not be content to be anything less than El Capitan in Yosemite, or the Grand Canyon. However, this concept misses the point provided by the beauty of the Old Testament poetry. God as a rock has holes in it in the Old Testament. He is so close to man that he provides a place for shelter, a place in which man can hide, a place that proves he cares, and a place where man can be nurtured. In addition, Scripture teaches again that man is only complete while he is in relationship with God. He becomes perfect in the Old Testament sense only in relationship with God. Genesis suggests this closeness in the phrase, ". . . Walk before me, and be perfect."[11]

Meaningful relationships with God become such only as God is seen interested in troubled lives. Counselors who fail to see the need for individuals' responses to God during reflective sessions with young searchers fail in their task as religious educators.

Methods useful here are those which provide a moratorium and rebirth. Retreats are an excellent means to focus in on this personal caring of God, and they form an important link with identity search, getting one away from the press of society and life itself and enhancing the chance for personal faith. Journal keeping is another method which can provide startling insight to religious quest. Meditation and prayer groups become therapeutic methods of personalizing religion, while celebrations and creative projects enrich the chance for God to touch the life. If we are in creative action, the mind symbolizes and organizes the meanings of life and religion in very personal terms. The symbols are drawn from the mind's concepts and because of that, provide a creative means of explaining God to man.

Theologians are trying Bible rewriting and story-telling as a creative means for personal insight into the community of faith. Developing a little story, like the journal writing suggested, can provide a unique chance for personal reflection. For, "to engage in telling one's 'little story' can be helpful in fitting it into the 'big story.' This enables a person to see his or her existence with an enhanced measure of coherent, historical meaning."[12] The obvious product of such activities suggested and guided by the counselor will enrich the reflection necessary for faith to have meaning. It will be their faith, then, and not mine which will sustain them through turmoil and their broken historical sense.

MATURITY AND BELONGING

This issue of maturity and belonging which a counselor dealing with youth must face in identity passage is especially important. Since personal identity formation as well as conversion's response as an identity function are age-related in part, it is necessary to encourage growth and movement in times of identity confusion for resolution to take place. This can be best done by visioning a better way.

Man has the capacity to see, if only in his mind's eye, how he "ought" to be. He can vision the future, he can make it live—if only in his imagination, it is so. This capacity for reaching beyond forms the basis for symbolizing and creativity in humankind. The counselor's responsibility here is to aid the individual in visioning the possibilities for his life. Growth and maturity are products of striving and stretching in the life. The Bible's use is significant here. Text after text can be presented as potential ways that one, in relationship with God, becomes whole. Suggestions to rewrite portions of Scripture which stretch man's values have a significant effect in the identity quest by providing the goals in religious life. For example, the discussion in I Corinthians 13 on love is an excellent concept, far above the normal way man loves. Love is here described as never rude and always longsuffering, and so on. The possibilities are beyond the mortal realm, except through a gift from God. Through the visioning and stretching process, using written and dialogical material, questors can find the direction for their lives. The goals become clarified because the target is clear. The goals in Scripture are somewhat idealistic, but nevertheless, no one will ever mature if they are not stretched to what they have not yet become. The results of this type of counseling methodology will be a sense of belonging. The sense comes through the counselors and the communities striving also to mature. The person learns that all are on a journey. No one has yet reached the end. The race is not over nor the prize on the mantleplace. He, too, has friends who are striving to become, and all need the stretching and visioning that religious faith provides. The counseling relationship then is not so designed to produce a type of product, but rather to equip a person to grow toward maturity in his religious experience and to sense a spirit to fit and join in being at home with God.

RELIGIOUS CHANGE

This last area of concern for the counselor comes when he is confronted with someone in the midst of making choices which will affect his or her religious life specifically. Those who come to us sensing the "call" of God in their lives are the ones who I am now talking about, and those who perhaps have never sensed the presence of God in their lives, but who are now sensing the nudging in their own psychological makeup and desire some clarification as to this pressure.

It is during these times of anxiety and often guilt that the religious counselor can provide a most necessary service and insight. Discussions which show God's deep care for the questor and illustrations regarding biblical individuals who were accepted by God, but yet still seemed to struggle to maintain a relationship, are important. Jonah, Abraham, Moses, Daniel, and even the New Testament Peter are all good examples of people coming to know God. The prophet Elijah's own experience with the still, small voice reflects moments of quiet meditation when new concepts and insights of God are most apt to occur, rather than in the hustle and bustle of fire and lightning.

Guilt is often the motivator for religious change, however, and it is this factor that sends many depressed people to counselors for help. Guilt is caused by the perception of a demand which is unable to be met, or through the condemnation—real or perceived—of another that their lives are out of harmony with that will of God. Often we superimpose guilt because we want people to do it our way. When this guilt is perceived, it is more or less real, and the anxiety is just as great, even though it has been produced by the wrong means.

The message religion has to provide to the world is one

of freedom from guilt and one of salvation and fit. Implicit within this message is the concept of forgiveness and hope. It is here that the community as counselor can be of great help in providing the reality of acceptance and identity.

The way the counselor and community handle their own anxiety and guilt may provide a clue to understanding how anxious seekers after God may find rest. This "living theology" becomes important. God must be presented as a God with whom we can be identified. The themes of Scripture which reinforce this can be good starting points for inductive study. The religious counselor may guide, sustain, reconcile, and assist the individual undergoing conviction for change through the use of passages and acceptance and forgiveness, hope and joy.

We all carry guilt for a number of reasons. Often the guilt is the product of man's own doing, as I have mentioned, and (a sense of) forgiveness is harder to obtain if the guilt is not deserved. Guidance to find identity in God, and with that the peaceful assurance of forgiveness is essential if man is to survive in a relational world. The individual who can rest in the assurance of God's forgiveness and grow to know the will of God will be better able to cope with a life confronted with anxiety. It is this sense of basic acceptance and oneness with God's will that is the essence of conversional return. The religious message to people that feel themselves misplaced and out of touch with reality is that there is a newness of mind that is available in religious return. The answers to the identity quest, the acceptance and at-homeness are available, and that belonging and stability are all resident in the community of believers. What must be made clear is that the life with God and man is a present reality and a real possibility, for with return to God comes peace. Peace is not just the presence of tranquility in the life. It is a sense of reconciliation and personal belonging in a sense of history. With peace comes surety and direction, and with a new direction, anxiety is eliminated. The religious conversion experience with its identity implications as well as the identity quest itself provides potential for the church's mission and a clarity of task like no other experience can provide.

NOTES

1. H. Richard Niebuhr, *The Meaning of Revelation* (New York: The Macmillan Co., 1962), pp. 63–65.

2. Ibid., p. 113.

3. Dugald S. Arbuckle, *Counseling: Philosophy, Theory and Practice* (Boston, Mass.: Allyn and Bacon, Inc., 1967), p. 24.

4. Paul Irwin, *The Care and Counseling of Youth in the Church* (Philadelphia, Penn.: Fortress Press, 1975), p. 56.

5. Howard J. Clinebell, Jr., *Basic Types of Pastoral Counseling* (Nashville, Tenn.: Abingdon Press, 1966), p. 19.

6. Quoted in ibid.

7. Larry Richards, *A Theology of Christian Education* (Michigan: Zondervan, 1976), p. 16.

8. Reuel Howe, *Man's Need and God's Action* (Greenwich, Conn.: The Seabury Press, Inc., 1953), p. 141.

9. Randolph Crump Miller, in *The Religious Education We Need*, ed. James M. Lee (Mishawaka, Ind.: Religious Education Press, 1977), p. 34.

10. Niebuhr, *Meaning of Revelation*, pp. 107–110.

11. Genesis 17:1.

12. Irwin, *Care and Counseling of Youth*, p. 67.

SUBJECT AND AUTHOR INDEX